Cambridge Primary Path 4

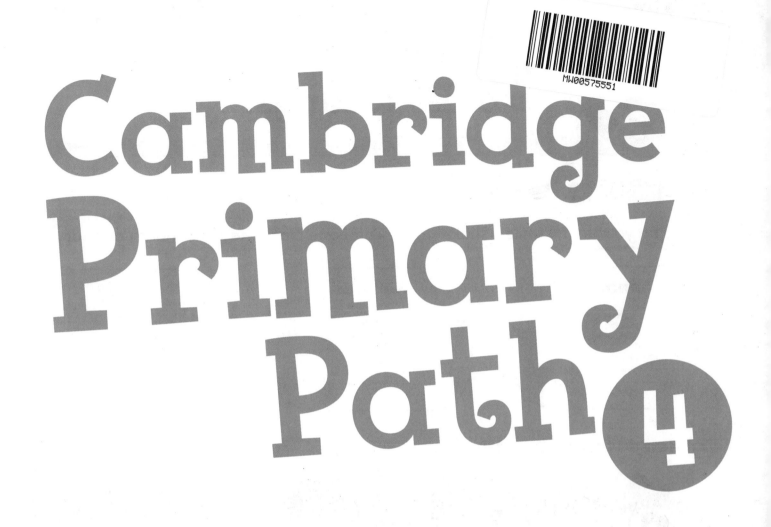

Activity Book

Helen Kidd

How do we express feelings?

1 Key Words 1 ▶ 1.1 **Watch the video. Complete the graphic organizer.**

> stomp your feet   smile   shake   drive someone crazy   laugh   mouth goes dry

Annoyed 😠	**Nervous** 😓	**Happy** 🙂
_____ _____	_____ _____	_____ _____

2 **How do they feel? Match.**

1

2

3

a   annoyed

b   upset

c   nervous

3 Key Words 1 **Complete.**

> shake   stomps her feet   apologize   smile   drives me crazy

a   It _____ when my brother takes my toys.

b   When I get nervous, my hands sometimes _____ .

c   When my little sister gets angry, she _____ .

d   It's better to _____ when you feel calm, not when you feel angry.

e   My dad's jokes always make me _____ !

1 Key Words 2 **Match.**

1 sweat   a   sad

2 scream   b   sudden, angry crying, often in a young child

3 pout   c   to produce liquid through your skin

4 hug   d   feeling pleased about something you did

5 unhappy   e   to push your lips forward, often to show you are annoyed

6 proud   f   to squeeze someone in your arms

7 tantrum   g   to make a long, loud, high sound

2 **Read and complete.**

> sweat   scream   pouts   hugged   unhappy   proud   tantrum

a My little brother got annoyed and had a big _____. He cried and stomped his feet.

b When you run around a lot or get nervous, you sometimes _____.

c "Are you OK? You look a little _____."

d The girls felt very _____ when they won the soccer tournament.

e Finn _____ his friend when his friend was upset.

f If you feel really angry, _____ at the sky rather than another person!

g My sister sometimes _____ if she doesn't get what she wants.

1 Look. What do you think the article is about?

2 Read. Circle the theme of the article.

a friends

b laughter

c health

Reading Strategy: Identifying Theme

The theme of a text is the most important message or topic. Identifying the theme can help you understand the text.

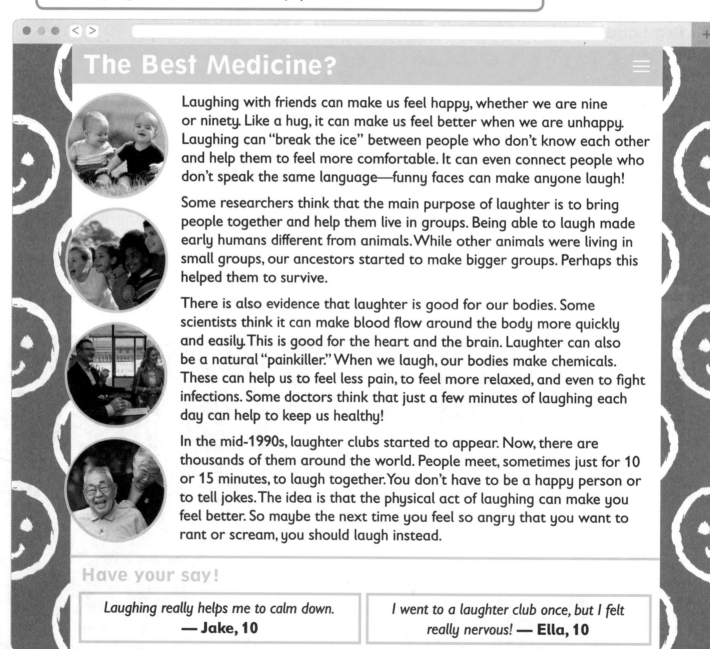

The Best Medicine?

Laughing with friends can make us feel happy, whether we are nine or ninety. Like a hug, it can make us feel better when we are unhappy. Laughing can "break the ice" between people who don't know each other and help them to feel more comfortable. It can even connect people who don't speak the same language—funny faces can make anyone laugh!

Some researchers think that the main purpose of laughter is to bring people together and help them live in groups. Being able to laugh made early humans different from animals. While other animals were living in small groups, our ancestors started to make bigger groups. Perhaps this helped them to survive.

There is also evidence that laughter is good for our bodies. Some scientists think it can make blood flow around the body more quickly and easily. This is good for the heart and the brain. Laughter can also be a natural "painkiller." When we laugh, our bodies make chemicals. These can help us to feel less pain, to feel more relaxed, and even to fight infections. Some doctors think that just a few minutes of laughing each day can help to keep us healthy!

In the mid-1990s, laughter clubs started to appear. Now, there are thousands of them around the world. People meet, sometimes just for 10 or 15 minutes, to laugh together. You don't have to be a happy person or to tell jokes. The idea is that the physical act of laughing can make you feel better. So maybe the next time you feel so angry that you want to rant or scream, you should laugh instead.

Have your say!

Laughing really helps me to calm down.
— **Jake, 10**

I went to a laughter club once, but I felt really nervous! — **Ella, 10**

SB pages 8–11

3 Mark ✓ the themes the article covers.

a the effect of laughter on our bodies ☐

b the purpose of laughter ☐

c how to make yourself laugh ☐

d how laughter makes us feel better ☐

e how to tell a good joke ☐

f early humans and laughter ☐

4 Read and circle *T* (true) or *F* (false).

a You can laugh only with people you know.   T F

b Laughter can connect people who speak different languages.   T F

c Only early humans, not animals, could laugh.   T F

d We feel pain more when we laugh.   T F

e Laughter clubs started in the 1990s.   T F

f At laughter clubs, people get together to tell jokes.   T F

5 What do you think? Read and answer.

a How do you feel when you laugh with friends?

_____

b What do you think of laughter clubs? Would you go to one?

_____

Interrupted Past

I started to sweat while I was waiting to give my presentation.
While you were sleeping, your phone rang!

The girl had a tantrum while her dad was shopping.
While other animals were living in small groups, our ancestors started to live in bigger groups.

1 Complete the sentences from the song on Student's Book page 12. Use the past simple or past progressive.

> look   read   play   break

a While I was staying at the beach, I _____ my smartphone.

b While I _____ on the beach, I lost my new shoes.

c I ate some ice cream while I _____ out to sea.

d I _____ my book while I was lying in the sun.

2 Complete. Use the past simple or past progressive.

a

While we _____ (play) in the park, it _____ (start) to rain.

b

While I _____ (think) about my vacation, I _____ (fall) asleep.

c

Lucy's dad _____ (sneeze) while they _____ (watch) TV.

d

While Oscar _____ (pack) his bag, he suddenly _____ (feel) nervous about the competition.

6

3 Look. Do you know the name of the man in the photo?

_____

4 Read and check. Then, complete with the correct form of the past simple or past progressive.

Mahatma Gandhi was a very famous Indian leader. He
1 _____ (believe) that all people should be
equal. But when he was a student, speaking in public
2 _____ (not / be) easy for him. Once, while he
3 _____ (give) a presentation to a group of people, he
4 _____ (feel) very nervous. He 5 _____ (not
/ can) speak. Someone else 6 _____ (finish) the presentation for him.
Another time, while he 7 _____ (work), he 8 _____ (leave)
a meeting because he was so nervous that he couldn't think of any questions to ask!

5 Make sentences with the past simple and past progressive.

a While / they / lie on the beach / the storm / start

_____

b While / I / have lunch / my cousins / arrive

_____

c Carla / feel / excited / while / she / go to the party

_____

d You / call / while / I / study

_____

e While / Dan / talk on the phone / the email arrive

_____

My Life

Finish the sentences with information about you. Use the past progressive.

a While I was thinking about _____ , I felt really excited.
b While I was _____ , I felt nervous.
c I felt annoyed while _____ .

1 **Say and write the words. Underline *ai*, *ay*, *ei*, or *ea*.**

_____

_____

_____

_____

_____

_____

2 **Circle the word with the different vowel sound.**

a	break	great	sweat
b	steak	react	break
c	protein	sleigh	eight
d	explain	say	scream
e	health	play	paint
f	wait	beach	stay

Oracy

1 **Read. Underline three useful ground rules for a discussion. Circle three useful ground rules for discussion and collaboration.**

- Listen to each other's ideas.
- Look up.
- Shout.

- Ask each other *What do you think?* and *Why?*
- Speak loudly.
- Speak quickly.

- Try to agree in the end.
- Speak clearly.
- Talk at the same time as other people.

Adjectives

When we talk about emotions, we often use *-ed* adjectives. These adjectives tell people how we feel about something.

I felt bored / frightened / excited.

When we describe things such as books, movies, or events, we often use *-ing* adjectives. These adjectives tell people about the the things that make us feel an emotion.

The movie was boring / frightening / exciting.

1 **Read and circle.**

a Did you go to bed late? You look really **tired / tiring**.

b They didn't like the movie—it was too **frightened / frightening.**

c The teacher was **annoyed / annoying** when the children didn't listen.

d I have some **excited / exciting** news—I won the art competition!

e What do you think is more **interested / interesting**—math or English?

f My mom is **bored / boring** with her job. She's looking for a new one.

2 **Read and complete with *-ed* or *-ing* forms of the words in the box.**

> tire   excite   bore   frighten   relax   interest

a Lily was so _____ about her vacation that she couldn't sleep.

b Sometimes, when I'm angry, I listen to _____ music.

c Tom is really _____ in photography—he loves it.

d "Did you like the book?" "Not much—I thought it was _____."

e Our cat is _____ of loud noises. She hides behind the sofa!

f I was so _____ that I slept through the movie!

1 READ **Answer the questions.**

How many lines do the writers use in each poem? Why?

poem 1: _____   poem 2: _____

friendsHip
    lAughs
loving Pets
        sPecial occasions
exciting daYs out

feeling fruStrated
    all ALone
    tearDrops fall

2 PLAN **Prepare to write an acrostic poem. Choose an emotion. Complete the graphic organizer.**

a   How many lines do you need to use? _____

b   Choose words and phrases you brainstormed in the Student's Book. Circle one letter in each line that is part of your emotion word. Select the best ones for your poem.

Hidden Emotion Word:
Words and Phrases:

3 WRITE **Use the graphic organizer to write your poem in your notebooks.**

4 EDIT **Did you ...**

☐ check the spelling of your emotion word?   ☐ include an *-ed* adjective?
☐ include an *-ing* adjective?

Ready to Read: Fiction

1 **Key Words 4** **Circle.**

1 I was so _____ when my presentation was finished. I could finally relax!

   a strict   b relieved   c shy

2 Jo really _____—she's the tallest in her class.

   a gets lost   b follows   c stands out

3 That was _____! We got the last two tickets for the concert.

   a lucky   b strict   c lost

4 How do you like to relax after a _____ day?

   a relieved   b stressful   c embarrassed

5 The soccer coach is very _____. We always do what she tells us.

   a strict   b lost   c stressful

6 Danny felt really _____ when he dropped his lunch on the floor.

   a relieved   b lucky   c embarrassed

2 **Find the words!**

embarrassed
stand out
stressful   lucky
strict   shy
courage   lost
relieved   follow

R	X	D	M	J	C	F	Y	Z	D	I	T
E	M	B	A	R	R	A	S	S	E	D	S
L	E	Q	D	R	N	M	L	T	E	W	H
I	R	L	X	U	S	L	U	C	K	Y	Y
E	W	P	S	G	T	O	F	S	K	O	B
V	A	N	O	N	D	M	S	W	D	J	R
E	W	U	Y	N	X	T	S	O	L	Y	M
D	Y	O	A	Y	C	J	E	N	B	H	V
T	H	T	L	E	G	A	R	U	O	C	O
E	S	A	F	L	I	S	T	R	I	C	T
O	R	L	I	D	O	R	S	X	Z	S	B
A	F	P	X	G	N	F	V	O	O	Y	V

1 **Look at the pictures and answer.**

   a Where do you think the story is set?_____

   b How do you think the boy feels? _____

2 **Read and check your answers to Activity I.**

Reading Strategy: Identifying Plot, Setting, and Character

It helps us understand a text if we know where the action happens (the setting), know who the people are (the characters), and can summarize what events happen (the plot).

A Special Certificate

Tim couldn't believe this was happening again. He felt hot, and he was starting to sweat. He looked around the school auditorium and tried to find something to look at to help him feel better. He stared though the tall windows at the sun and the bright blue sky. It made him think of vacations in the mountains. He relaxed a little and felt relieved.

But when he remembered where he was, he felt nervous again. Now his mouth felt dry, too. Every Friday, in a Celebration Assembly, the principal, Mr. Anderson, presented certificates—usually for doing well in sports or music or for doing good work in class. Most children loved going up on stage to get a certificate, but Tim didn't like it at all. He was shy, and for him, it was very stressful.

Tim listened to the names—"Freddie Lewis … Anna Matthews …"—and he knew his name might come soon. He didn't want to feel embarrassed in front of the whole school again.

"If he calls my name, I'll run away. Then, I won't have to go up." he thought to himself.

"The next certificate I have is for Tim Orlando, in fifth grade." Too late!

Everyone started clapping. Tim wanted to disappear. He remembered his teacher's advice and took a deep breath. "Everyone gets nervous sometimes," he thought. His friend Pablo smiled at him. "You can do this," he said.

Tim stood up and walked up to the stage. As he took the certificate from Mr. Anderson, his hands were still shaking.

"This certificate," said Mr. Anderson, smiling, "is for working hard to stay calm and for having the courage to come up onto the stage and receive it."

3 **Complete a story map.**

Main character: _____

Other characters: _____

Where does the action happen? _____

What happens? _____

_____

Beginning: _____

_____

Middle: _____

_____

End: _____

_____

4 **Read again and circle _T_ (true) or _F_ (false).**

a It was sunny outside.   **T**   **F**

b When Tim looked out of the window, he felt better.   **T**   **F**

c The story is set on a Monday.   **T**   **F**

d Tim was surprised when the principal said his name.   **T**   **F**

e Tim thought about running away before he got his certificate.   **T**   **F**

f Tim doesn't have any friends.   **T**   **F**

5 **Read and answer.**

a What makes you feel nervous?

_____

_____

b What advice would you give to a nervous friend?

You should _____.

You shouldn't _____.

First Conditional

If he calls my name, **I'll** run away.
If you don't like your present, **I'll** return it to the store.
We **won't** go to the park **if** it rains tomorrow.
They **won't** play well as a team **if** they don't practice together.

1 **Complete with *'ll (will)* or *won't*.**

a

If you play the piano, I _____ play the violin.

b

It _____ drive your sister crazy if you take her clothes.

c

If he falls asleep, he _____ see the movie!

d

They _____ go to the party if they don't finish their homework.

2 **Match.**

1 If it's sunny tomorrow,
2 If I have to perform on stage,
3 If we arrive home late,
4 If they don't run,
5 If you remember to breathe slowly,
6 If we don't study for the test,

a there won't be time to watch TV.
b the teacher will be annoyed.
c you won't feel so nervous.
d I'll feel nervous.
e we won't stay indoors.
f they won't catch the bus!

14

3 Complete to make first conditional sentences.

a   If I _____ (see) a turtle, I _____ (take) a photo.

b   He _____ (be) hungry later if he _____ (not eat) now.

c   If we _____ (lose) the game, I _____ (be) sad.

d   If they _____ (not score) another goal, they _____ (not win).

e   You _____ (not pass) your exam if you _____ (not practice).

f   If she _____ (not clean) her room, it _____ (drive) Mom crazy.

4 Write first conditional sentences.

a   if / she / win   she / get a gold medal

_____

b   if / I / not have time   I / not go shopping

_____

c   you / feel better   if / you / apologize

_____

d   they / not be happy   if / we / not go to the party

_____

e   if / I / wear that hat   I / feel embarrassed

_____

f   you / not get lost   if / you / follow the signs

_____

5 Complete to make first conditional sentences that are true for you.

a   If it rains on the weekend, _____

_____.

b   If we don't go on vacation, _____

_____.

c   If I don't _____

_____.

d   If I _____

_____.

Values: Being a Good Friend

1 **What is being a good friend? Read and circle.**

5 = a very good friend   1 = not a very good friend

	A good friend?
Being honest	👍 👍 👍 👍 👍
Apologizing when you do something wrong	👍 👍 👍 👍 👍
Competing with your friends all the time	👍 👍 👍 👍 👍
Doing the things you say you will do	👍 👍 👍 👍 👍
Using kind language	👍 👍 👍 👍 👍
Talking all the time	👍 👍 👍 👍 👍

2 **Who is being a good friend? Look and mark ✓.**

I'm really sorry I'm late!

Are you OK?

3 **Why is being a good friend important?**

_____

_____

_____

16

Check Your Oracy!

1 My group followed the ground rules for discussion. **All the time / Sometimes / Never**

2 Were any ground rules broken? **Yes / No**

3 If any ground rules were broken, which one(s)?

_____

The Big Challenge

How can we show respect for our classmates' feelings?

1 **Color the stars to give yourself a score.***

I thought of ideas for our class contract.	☆☆☆☆☆
I worked with my group to share and choose our ideas.	☆☆☆☆☆
I helped to write the ideas on our poster.	☆☆☆☆☆
I helped to design and illustrate our poster.	☆☆☆☆☆
I practiced presenting our poster with my group.	☆☆☆☆☆
I presented our poster with my group.	☆☆☆☆☆

*(5 = Awesome! 4 = Pretty good, 3 = OK, 2 = Could be better, I = Needs more work!)

2 **Whose poster did you like best?** _____

3 **What did you like most about it?** _____

_____

The Big Question and **Me**

Because of the things I have learned in this unit,

1 I will _____ .

2 I will _____ .

1 Complete with a word.

> drives me crazy   nervous   apologized   stomp your feet   smile

a After I shouted, I _____ to my friend.

b Luisa, please don't _____ when you get angry.

c When you feel _____, remember to breathe!

d The sound of buzzing insects _____.

e When Nick saw his friend _____, he felt better.

2 Circle.

1 When I was angry, I wanted to _____.

  a scream **b** sweat **c** hug

2 Counting to ten can give you time to _____.

  a rant **b** pout **c** calm down

3 There's a part of your brain that _____ to anger.

  a reacts **b** rants **c** pulls

4 Ben felt very _____ when he passed his piano exam.

  a annoyed **b** proud **c** unhappy

5 You should _____ your friend—she looks sad.

  a sweat **b** hug **c** pout

3 Complete.

> lost   relieved   strict   follow   courage

a We always listen in class—our teacher is very _____.

b You need _____ to do things that make you nervous.

c Oh, no—we're _____! I don't know where we are!

d _____ me—I'll show you where the classroom is.

e I'm so _____ that the test is finshed! I can relax now.

4) Make sentences with the past simple and past progressive.

a It / start to rain / while / the boys / play basketball

_____

b While / we / watch the movie / Dad / fall asleep!

_____

c My phone / ring / while / I / cook dinner

_____

d While / Sara / listen to the music / she / want to cry

_____

5) Complete with the correct form of the verbs to make first conditional sentences.

a If they _____ (finish) early, they _____ (go) to the park.

b If it _____ (be) sunny, we _____ (order) an ice cream.

c If he _____ (not study), he _____ (not get) a good grade.

d I _____ (hug) my friend if she _____ (be) sad.

e Ella _____ (not go) swimming if she _____ (not find) her swimsuit!

f They _____ (not make) the soccer team if they _____ (not practice) every week.

6) Complete with the *-ed* or *-ing* form of the word in parentheses.

a Wow! That's an _____ (amaze) view!

b I was really _____ (surprise) when I heard your news.

c My friend has a really _____ (annoy) habit—he bites his nails.

d They weren't very _____ (interest) in watching TV.

e Are you _____ (frighten) of the dark? You should leave a light on.

f Wow! That was a really_____ (tire) day.

SPEAKING MISSION

1 **What did they say? Complete the conversation.**

> feeling   don't   course   can   wrong   sorry   shouldn't   what if

Charlotte	Why are you crying? What's 1 _____?
Ivy	I feel sad.
Charlotte	Why are you 2 _____ sad?
Ivy	We're moving to a different neighborhood.
Charlotte	I'm 3 _____ about that.
Ivy	I have to start a new school. I feel nervous and anxious thinking about it.
Charlotte	4 _____ you talk to your parents?
Ivy	I already have ... They said it's because my mom got a new job. We need to be closer to her work.
Charlotte	Why 5 _____ you get to know the new neighborhood?
Ivy	Good idea. Dad said it's closer to the beach.
Charlotte	Well, that's good news! I can come and visit! We can go swimming.
Ivy	I'd really like that. But 6 _____ I don't like the school?
Charlotte	You 7 _____ worry. You should think of it as an adventure.
Ivy	I feel scared. What if I don't make any friends?
Charlotte	Of 8 _____ you will.

2 **Match.**

1	What's	a	should ...
2	Why are you	b	talk to ...?
3	Can you	c	don't you ...?
4	Why	d	wrong?
5	You	e	feeling (sad)?

3 **What can someone do to make new friends? Write two things.**

_____

_____

What can you remember about ... Unit 1?

1 **What is she doing? Circle.**

apologizing
calming down
stomping her foot

2 **What might someone do when they are nervous? Mark ✓ two things.**

pout ☐ shake ☐ sweat ☐

3 **What are they doing? Underline.**

They are **ranting / hugging / screaming**.

4 **Complete.**

My brother's so annoying—he drives me _____!

5 **How does he feel? Circle.**

He feels really **embarrassed / shy / relieved** because the test is over.

6 **Complete.**

"Oh, no! This is the wrong place. We're _____!"

7 **What happened to the boy from the song in the Student's Book? Complete.**

While he _____ on the beach, he _____.

8 **Complete the advice. Use a first conditional sentence.**

If you _____ (talk) about your emotions, you _____ (feel) happier.

Read and underline.

9 "Why are you so tired / tiring?"

10 "I couldn't sleep because I was so excited / exciting about the trip."

Check your answers in the Student's Book. How did you do?
10 ☐ Wow! 8–9 ☐ Great! 6–7 ☐ Good! 0–5 ☐ Try harder!

? 😃 **How do we express feelings?** Write your answer to the Big Question.

_____
_____

2 What can space exploration teach us?

1 Key Words 1 ▶ 2.1 **Watch the video. Complete the graphic organizer.**

> Milky Way scientific experiments constellations space probes
> observe GPS Space Station

_____,
for example, Voyager I
Travel really far
(e.g., to Jupiter
and Saturn)
No people
on board

**How can
we explore
space?**

International
_____
Travels around the Earth
People live on
board—
do _____

Satellites
Travel around the Earth
Send back lots of useful
information about
weather,
TV signals, maps,
_____

Telescopes
_____
from Earth
Can see _____
of stars, planets,
the _____

2 **Complete.**

> observe constellations Space Station GPS gravity

a People work, eat, and sleep on the International _____.

b There is no _____ in space.

c _____ are patterns of stars.

d We use _____ satellites when we need a map.

e _____ is another word for *look closely*.

Ready to Read: Nonfiction

1 Key Words 2 **Match.**

1	solar system	a	a vehicle that travels in space
2	launch	b	a person who travels in space
3	satellite	c	to send something into space (or water)
4	astronaut	d	the outside or top part of something
5	planet	e	an object sent into space to collect information
6	spacecraft	f	the sun and eight planets that travel around it
7	surface	g	Earth, for example

2 **Circle.**

a The sun is at the center of our **planet** / **solar system**.

b Neptune is the furthest **planet** / **spacecraft** in our solar system.

c When I'm older, I want to be **a satellite** / **an astronaut**.

d The **satellite** / **surface** sent a lot of information back to Earth.

e Russia was the first country to **launch** / **land** a dog into space.

f Do you think you could live on **an astronaut** / **a spacecraft**?

g I wonder what the **surface** / **solar system** of Mars feels like.

1 **Look. What do you think the article is about?** _____

2 **Read. Mark ✓ the four main ideas in the article.**

where astronauts come from ☐   planning meals for space ☐

eating in space ☐   space food now and in the past ☐

types of food in space ☐   getting clean in space ☐

Reading Strategy: Main Idea and Details

The main idea is what a text is about. The details support the main idea and add extra information.

What Do Astronauts Eat?

Would you like to eat your lunch from a tube, like a toothpaste tube? In the early days of space travel, that's what astronauts had to do. Then, scientists invented a special way to prepare and store food for space travel by cooking, freezing, and drying it. Now, luckily, space food is much tastier! It's more like the food we eat on Earth.

The International Space Station (ISS) is a satellite that orbits the Earth. Astronauts live and work there for around six months at a time. They come from the U.S.A., Russia, Japan, Canada, and Europe. The food they enjoy on board is similar to the food in their own countries—like chicken and rice, Russian soup, or Dutch cheese.

Astronauts' bodies work differently in space because there is no gravity. They need to keep themselves healthy on board. Meal planners work with the astronauts before they go into space. The astronauts choose from a list of more than 100 tasty and nutritious foods— including spaghetti and fruit salad. Then, the meal planners prepare the food, put it into small plastic bags, and lock each meal in a special tray.

Eating in space is different from eating on Earth. The astronauts have to add water to the food before they can eat it. Then, they have to tie their food to the table or their legs to stop it from floating away! No gravity also means that the astronauts can't smell their food—the smell often disappears before it reaches their noses!

Could you be an astronaut? Before you answer, there's something else you should know: astronauts can even make pizza and eat ice cream in space now! Does that help you decide?!

3 Write the four main ideas from Activity 2 in the chart.

Main Idea	Detail 1	Detail 2
Paragraph 1		
Paragraph 2		
Paragraph 3		
Paragraph 4		

4 Underline two details for each main idea in the article. Then, complete the chart with the ideas below.

Scientists invented a better way of preparing food.

Astronauts on the ISS come from many different countries.

Astronauts in space can't smell their food.

Meal planners help astronauts to choose tasty, nutritious food.

Space food is much tastier now than in the past.

It isn't easy to eat in space because there is no gravity.

On the ISS, astronauts eat food like their food from home.

Astronauts choose their food before they go into space.

5 Read and write.

a Write three countries that astronauts on the ISS come from.

_____   _____   _____

b Write three foods astronauts can eat in space.

_____   _____   _____

c Write two things that happen because there is no gravity in space.

_____

_____

Reflexive Pronouns: *myself, yourself, himself, herself, itself, yourselves, ourselves, themselves*

We use reflexive pronouns when the subject and object of the verb are the same.

I sometimes talk to myself.
Wow! Did you paint that yourself?
The baby laughed when she saw herself **in the mirror.**
My brother walks to school by himself.
The satellite destroyed itself **in space.**
We can cook this ourselves.
Be careful—don't hurt yourselves!
Astronauts need to keep themselves **healthy on board.**

1 **Complete.**

> myself   ourselves   yourself   themselves   himself   herself

a He likes to look at _____ in the mirror.

b Did you do your homework _____?

c I baked this cake _____.

d Astronauts wear special helmets to protect _____ in space.

e The astronaut taught _____ to speak Russian.

f Let's make a fire to keep _____ warm!

2 **Complete with a subject pronoun (*I, you, he, she, it, we, they*).**

a Why don't _____ do it yourself?

b Look! _____ made this model rocket myself.

c The computer is broken. _____ turned itself off.

d _____ cuts her hair herself.

e _____ did the whole project ourselves.

f _____ tries to keep himself fit on the space station.

g _____ zipped themselves into their spacesuits.

3 Complete with a reflexive pronoun.

a The astronauts saw _____ on TV.

b My dad taught _____ to swim.

c "Hi, girls. Did you enjoy _____ at the party?"

d We did scientific experiments on _____ while we were in space.

e I'm wearing sunscreen to protect _____ .

f The space probe destroyed _____ when it crashed.

4 Rewrite the sentences with *by* and a reflexive pronoun.

a
Tom practices basketball alone.

Tom _____ .

b
Did you make that without help?

Did you _____ ?

c
I did my homework on my own.

I _____ .

d
Sara and Carla learned to play the guitar without a teacher.

Sara and Carla _____ .

My Life

Read and answer. Write sentences with reflexive pronouns.

a Write one thing you couldn't do for yourself when you were a baby.

_____

b Write one unusual thing you did by yourself in the last year.

_____

1 **Say and write the words. Underline ee or ea.**

2 **Circle the word with the different vowel sound.**

a	pea	head	bee
b	steak	meat	beans
c	please	cheese	health

d	sweat	sweet	feet
e	scream	break	between
f	tea	beach	great

Oracy

1 **Read. Underline three phrases that ask for the views of other group members. Circle two phrases that recognize and respect the views of other group members.**

Jack Do you think it would get boring in space?

Kate Yes, of course it would. Imagine being in a spaceship all day and night. You wouldn't be able to go play soccer outside. You couldn't go bike riding with friends! I would go crazy. What do you think, Liam? Do you agree?

Liam Not really. I think it would be really awesome to be an astronaut. You could explore the planets and look down on Earth. Floating around in space would be amazing!

Kate Yes, but how long would that be fun for? Maybe a week at the most!

Jack That's a good point. And I would really miss skateboarding.

Definite and Indefinite Articles

We use indefinite articles (*a*/*an*) when we are mentioning something for the first time or talking about something that's not specific. We use *a* before words starting with a consonant and *an* before words starting with a vowel (*a, e, i, o, u*).

We use the definite article (*the*) when we and our listener/reader already know which specific thing we're talking about—either because we've already mentioned it or because there is only one of it (e.g., with superlative adjectives). We also use it with the names of mountain ranges, rivers, seas, oceans, and groups of islands or stars.

A space probe is different from a **spacecraft.**
Valentina Teryshkova was an **astronaut.**
Valentina Teryshkova was the **first woman in space.**

1) **Read and circle.**

a   We use **a / an** satellite phone to talk to scientists.

b   NASA is **a / the** National Aeronautics and Space Administration.

c   Oh, no! We have **a / the** problem with the phone!

d   Jupiter is **a / the** biggest planet.

e   I can see **a / the** Milky Way through the telescope.

f   Look! There's **a / an** asteroid!

2) **Read and complete with *a*, *an*, or *the*.**

Sally Ride was I _____ astronaut and astrophysicist. She was 2 _____ first American woman to travel in space, in 1983, on 3 _____ space shuttle *Challenger*. When she retired from space travel, she became director of 4 _____ California Space Institute at 5 _____ University of California. She also started 6 _____ company to encourage girls to study science and math.

1 READ **Answer the question.**

What two things does the writer think are amazing?

_____

_____

My Journal | **July 21**

This morning, I went for my first spacewalk. I had to go outside to fix a problem with the space station. Jessica and I went together. I loved being out in space—it was completely quiet. The view of Earth in the sunlight was beautiful! I could see clouds and the ocean. It was amazing. We quickly fixed the problem and came back inside for lunch.

Lunch was dried meat and noodles today. I think I prefer meals on Earth! After that, I did some exercise in the space gym.

It's difficult to stay fit and strong when there is no gravity, so I'm going to do two hours in the gym every day while I'm here.

For the rest of the day, I was working on scientific experiments. We talk to scientists back on Earth by using a satellite phone. It's pretty amazing. Yesterday, I used the satellite phone to speak to my children.

I hope I sleep better tonight. My body clock is confused because the sun rises and sets 16 times a day on the International Space Station! Also, sleeping without a bed is really weird.

2 PLAN **Prepare to write a journal entry about another day on the ISS. Complete the graphic organizer. Use at least two adjectives in each section.**

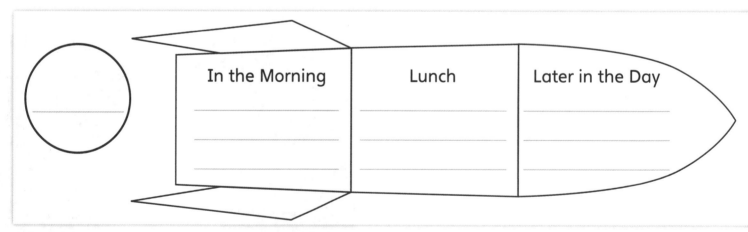

In the Morning

Lunch

Later in the Day

3 WRITE **Use the graphic organizer to write your journal entry in your notebooks.**

4 EDIT **Did you ...**

- ☐ include the date?
- ☐ write in the first person?
- ☐ use adjectives?
- ☐ use articles correctly?

1 Key Words 4 **Complete the crossword.**

Down

1 This is circle-shaped.

2 A feeling, when something doesn't go well.

3 Change words into a different language.

4 Everything that exists.

5 This keeps you safe in a car.

Across

1 The Milky Way is one of these.

2 Don't drink this! It will harm you.

3 This is a rock that flies around the sun.

4 Balloons and boats can do this.

5 There is no gravity here.

2 **Complete.**

translate   seatbelt   galaxy   float   rings   disappointed

a Tom was really _____ with his grade on the test. He got 4 out of 10.

b Can you help me to _____ this into English?

c Our _____ is a large group of stars and planets that includes the solar system.

d Astronauts _____ in space because there is no gravity.

e Fasten your _____ — it's time to go!

f The _____ around Saturn are made of ice.

1. **Look at the pictures and answer.**

   a   How do you think the astronauts feel? _____

   b   What do you think they are doing? _____

2. **Read and check your answers to Activity I.**

> **Reading Strategy: Predicting from Pictures**
>
> We can use pictures to help us predict what a text will be about. This makes it easier to read a new text.

Just the Right Balance

Finn took a deep breath. He checked his seatbelt again. And again. He had a lot of flying experience—in planes and spacecraft. But even after three space flights, he still got nervous just before they launched. And this flight was different. He was going farther than ever before, for longer than ever before. Finn was part of a mission to find out if humans could live and work on Mars.

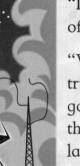

"Do you think we'll actually be able to land?" he asked Lucia, one of the other astronauts.

"We know it's possible," she said. "We just have to stay calm and trust ourselves. It's not like the outer planets—they're just balls of gas. And Mercury is too hot, Venus is hotter than Mercury, and there's poison in the atmosphere on Venus. But *Curiosity* already landed on Mars, so we can, too."

Just then, a low rumbling noise started and the whole spacecraft began to shake. Ten seconds later, it felt like an enormous kick. This was the most powerful launch vehicle ever. For two minutes, the noise and the shaking were incredible, until there was an enormous bang and the rocket motors fell off. Then, it became much smoother, although Finn still felt like there was an elephant sitting on him. Four minutes later, very suddenly, it felt like the elephant disappeared. They were beyond the Earth's atmosphere and in outer space. Finn started to float around.

"Wow! It's amazing every time," said Finn, as he stared down at Earth. The blue and green looked so deep and bright that he almost had to close his eyes. He hoped it wasn't the last time he saw Earth …

32

3 **Read again and circle *T* (true) or *F* (false).**

a   This is Finn's fourth trip into space.   T   F

b   Mercury and Venus are hotter than Earth.   T   F

c   It's very quiet inside the spacecraft.   T   F

d   The "elephant" suddenly disappeared because
they left the Earth's atmosphere.   T   F

e   The astronauts can't see anything outside the spacecraft.   T   F

f   Finn doesn't like living on Earth.   T   F

4 **Read and answer.**

a   Why does Finn get more nervous than usual on this flight?

_____

b   Why can't the spacecraft land on the outer planets?

_____

c   Why did the spacecraft stop shaking after two minutes?

_____

5 **What do you think?**

a   Why does the Earth look blue and green
from space?

_____

_____

b   Do you think people will live on Mars in
the future? Why or why not?

_____

_____

c   Would you like to go on a mission to
Mars? Why or why not?

_____

_____

_____

_____

Comparatives with -er, more, less, and than

Venus is hotter than **Mercury.**
Mars is drier than **Earth.**
I think space is more **beautiful** than **Earth.**
Life on the ISS is less **comfortable** than **life on Earth!**

1 **Circle.**

a Jupiter is **bigger / more big** than Saturn.

b The temperature on Earth is **comfortabler / more comfortable** than the temperature on Venus.

c The countryside is **less busy / more busy** than the city.

d What do you think is **more popular / popular**—soccer or basketball?

e Yum! This pizza is **more tasty / tastier** than my mom's.

2 **Look and complete with a comparative adjective + than. Choose from the words in parentheses.**

Neil Armstrong, Buzz Aldrin, and Michael Collins were the three astronauts on board the Apollo II mission—the first mission to land a spacecraft on the surface of the moon, in July 1969.

	Neil Armstrong	Buzz Aldrin	Michael Collins
Birthday	August 5, 1930	January 20, 1930	October 31, 1930
Height	1.8 m	1.78 m	1.8 m

a Buzz Aldrin was _____ Neil Armstrong and Michael Collins. (old / young)

b Michael Collins was _____ Neil Armstrong and Buzz Aldrin. (old / young)

c Neil Armstrong was _____ Buzz Aldrin but was _____ Michael Collins. (old / young)

d Neil Armstrong and Michael Collins were _____ Buzz Aldrin. (tall / short)

e Buzz Aldrin was _____ Neil Armstrong and Michael Collins. (tall / short)

3 Complete with a comparative adjective.

a Good news! This week's homework is a lot _____ (easy) than last week's.

b Alex is always smiling. She's _____ (happy) than her sister.

c The rainforest is _____ (wet) than the desert.

d I felt very calm before my test—much _____ (nervous) than last time.

e I prefer living in the countryside. It's _____ (peaceful) than the city.

f You'll love this book—it's much _____ (interesting) than the other one.

4 Rewrite the sentences with the same meaning. Use *less* + adjective.

a My mom was more annoyed than my dad.

My dad _____.

b Pablo is friendlier than Daniel.

Daniel _____.

c Antarctica is icier than Africa.

Africa _____.

d I think science is more interesting than English.

I think English _____.

e The children were more excited than the adults.

The adults _____.

f In my country, summer is sunnier than winter.

In my country, winter _____.

5 Complete to make true sentences for you. Use comparatives.

a _____ is more frightening than _____.

b _____ is less interesting than _____.

c _____ exciting _____.

d _____ (easy).

e _____ (sad).

1 **What is being a citizen of the world? Read and write *Yes* or *No*.**

	Does a citizen of the world do this?	Do I do this?
Learning about history		
Watching the news and reading newspapers or news websites		
Never visiting new places		
Being polite and showing respect to people from other cultures		
Learning another language		
Listening to music in other languages		

2 **Who is being a citizen of the world? Look and mark ✓.**

a I'm trying to learn more about other cultures. Is your culture important to you? ☐

b I believe that all people are equal. ☐

c I don't care where my food comes from. ☐

d I want to travel to another country and work there. ☐

e Reading about other countries is boring. ☐

f I like to visit my library to find books about world history and events. ☐

3 **Why is being a citizen of the world important?**

_____

_____

_____

_____

_____

Check Your Oracy!

1 I participated in the discussion. **All the time / Sometimes / Never**

2 I listened to and respected my classmates' ideas. **All the time / Sometimes / Never**

3 If someone had a different opinion, were the group members respectful? **Yes / No**

How can we design a machine to explore space?

The Big Challenge

1 **Color the stars to give yourself a score.***

I researched some famous spacecrafts online.	☆☆☆☆☆
I thought of some ideas and shared them with my group.	☆☆☆☆☆
I helped design the spacecraft with my group.	☆☆☆☆☆
I helped to make and label our poster.	☆☆☆☆☆
I practiced presenting our poster with my group.	☆☆☆☆☆
I presented our poster with my group.	☆☆☆☆☆

*(5 = Awesome! 4 = Pretty good, 3 = OK, 2 = Could be better, 1 = Needs more work!)

2 **Whose poster did you like best?**

_____

3 **What did you like most about it?**

_____

The Big Question and Me

Because of the things I have learned in this unit,

1 I will _____.

2 I will _____.

37

1 Circle.

a People stay on the **space station** / **space probe** for around six months.

b You can use a telescope to **orbit** / **observe** the stars.

c A **space probe** / **Milky Way** traveled to Jupiter.

d Scientists study the effects of no **GPS** / **gravity** in space.

e Astronauts do a lot of **constellations** / **scientific experiments**.

f The **Milky Way** / **GPS** contains billions of stars.

2 Complete.

> surface   landed   solar system   orbit   launched   planets

a Earth is part of the _____.

b Mars and Jupiter are _____.

c Neil Amstrong walked on the _____ of the moon.

d NASA _____ the *Cassini* spacecraft in 1997.

e The *Curiosity Rover* _____ on Mars in 2012.

f Satellites _____ the Earth (or other planets).

3 Complete.

1 The ____ is everything there is.

   a galaxy   **b** asteroid   **c** universe

2 Don't eat that—it's ____!

   a poison   **b** rings   **c** space

3 I hope the ____ doesn't hit Earth.

   a universe   **b** seatbelt   **c** asteroid

4 Astronauts' ____ help to keep them safe in space.

   a seatbelts   **b** rings   **c** poison

5 A ____ contains billions of stars and planets.

   a satellite   **b** galaxy   **c** asteroid

4 **Complete with a reflexive pronoun.**

Astronauts on the ISS have to spend a lot of time doing scientific experiments on 1 _____. The British astronaut Tim Peake spent six months on the ISS in 2016. He did experiments on 2 _____ to find out about the effects of space travel on his skin, blood, bones, and breathing. He sent photos of 3 _____ washing and brushing his teeth! When U.S. astronaut Catherine (Cady) Coleman was on the ISS in 2011, she sent photos of 4 _____ playing the flute! Would you like to do scientific experiments on 5 _____?

5 **Complete with a comparative.**

a The Atacama Desert is _____ the Sahara Desert. It's the driest place in the world! (dry)

b Astronauts often lose weight in space. When they come back, they are often _____ before. (thin)

c My sister's _____ me—she always gets good grades on tests! (lucky)

d Traveling in space is _____ traveling on Earth. In fact, it's uncomfortable. (comfortable)

e I think being in the dark is _____ being in a small space. The dark really scares me. (frightening)

f I think English is _____ math. It's my favorite subject. (interesting)

6 **Read and complete with *a*, *an*, or *the*.**

a Uranus is _____ cold planet.

b Neptune is _____ coldest planet.

c Helen Sharman is _____ astronaut from the U.K.

d Yuri Gagarin was _____ first astronaut to travel into space.

e Apollo was _____ American space program.

f Is Pluto _____ planet or not?

SPEAKING MISSION

1 **What did they say? Complete the conversations.**

> title   sale   on   take   by   cover   author   discount   original   on sale

Sylvia Do you have any books
1 _____ space
2 _____ George Cousins?

Bookstore assistant Let me see ...
Yes, we have one down here.
Follow me ...

Bookstore assistant Here you go.

Sylvia Is it on 3 _____ ?

Bookstore assistant Let's look on the
front 4 _____ . Yes, it is!
Look, it's 15% off its
5 _____ price.

Sylvia How much is it with the
6 _____ ?

Bookstore assistant It's $22 with
the discount.

Sylvia Great. I'll take it!

Sylvia Do you have any books by ... oh ... I
don't remember the name of the
7 _____ . It's a book on the solar
system.

Bookstore assistant Can you remember the
8 _____ ?

Sylvia The title is something like ... *Wonders of
Our Solar System*.

Bookstore assistant I know the one. It is on
our discount table just behind you.

Sylvia Oh, that's it! *The Wonders of Our Solar
System*!

Bookstore assistant And you are in luck. It's
9 _____ .

Sylvia It says here it's $30.

Bookstore assistant But on sale, it's only $15!

Sylvia Amazing! I'll 10 _____ it.

2 **Match.**

1 The title is something like
2 I don't remember the name of the
3 It's a book about / on
4 Is it
5 Is there
6 Yes, there is a
7 I'll take

a a discount?
b it.
c 30% discount.
d space.
e *Wonders of Our Solar System*.
f on sale?
g author.

What can you remember about ... Unit 2?

(1) **What is this?**

_____

_____

(2) **What is the name for a group of stars?**

_____

(3) **What is it doing? Circle.**

landing
launching
orbiting

(4) **Circle.**

A **space probe / solar system / satellite** is a spacecraft that travels around a planet.

(5) **What is he/she doing? Mark ✓.**

floating ☐   orbiting ☐
translating ☐

(6) **What are these?**

_____

(7) **Complete with a reflexive pronoun.**

Astronauts need to keep
_____ healthy on
board the ISS.

(8) **Complete with a comparative.**

Earth is _____
Mercury. (big)

Read and circle.

(9) **Venus is a / the hottest planet.**

(10) **I saw a / an asteroid yesterday.**

Check your answers in the Student's Book. How did you do?

10 ☐ Wow!   8–9 ☐ Great!   6–7 ☐ Good!   0–5 ☐ Try harder!

(?) 😃 **What can space exploration teach us?** Write your answer to the Big Question.

_____

_____

_____

3 Is technology good or bad?

1) ▶ 3.1 **Watch the video. Complete the graphic organizer.**

a It allows us to connect to people all around the world immediately.
b Technology can be addictive.
c We are forgetting how to talk to each other.
d It can help us understand what is wrong with people and fix medical problems.
e The Internet lets us find information quickly and easily.
f Too much time on screens and mobile devices could be bad for our health.
g It might make our transportation faster and safer.
h Robots might start doing people's jobs.

Technology

Benefits / Advantages	Risks / Disadvantages
_____	_____
_____	_____
_____	_____
_____	_____

2) Key Words 1 **Complete.**

Internet   screens   inventions   allow   connect   search engine

a Some _____ have really changed the world.
b You can find information about lots of different things on the _____ .
c If you have a question, you can just type it into a _____ .
d We can _____ to people all over the world by email.
e Do we spend too much time looking at _____ ?
f _____ is another word for *let*.

1 Key Words 2   **Match.**

1	app	a	a cell phone that connects to the Internet
2	animation	b	a small flying robot
3	drone	c	a machine that measures changes in something
4	program	d	all the instructions that control a computer
5	sensor	e	moving pictures made from drawings or models
6	smartphone	f	to write a set of instructions that make a computer do something
7	software	g	a small computer program that you download onto a mobile device

2 **Circle.**

1 I have a great new _____ on my phone.

   a drone   **b** software   **b** app

2 Our car can park itself—it has special _____.

   a sensors   **b** animations   **b** selfies

3 Look! I made this _____ on my phone.

   a manufacturer   **b** drone   **b** animation

4 The _____ in driverless cars communicates with other cars.

   a drone   **b** software   **b** selfies

5 Do you think you could _____ a robot?

   a program   **b** connect   **b** allow

6 In the future, _____ might deliver our groceries.

   a sensors   **b** drones   **b** animations

1 **Look. What do you think the article is about?** _____

2 **Read. Circle the best summary of the article.**

a   Adults are better inventors than children.

b   Inventors can be any age and from anywhere.

c   Good inventors always get things right.

Reading Strategy: Identifying Main Idea and Details

The main idea of a paragraph is normally supported by details. Often, the main idea can be found in the first sentence.

What's Your Big Idea?

Have you heard of Thomas Edison? His most famous inventions have helped play important parts in our lives—electric lighting, a type of movie camera, and a "talking machine" that recorded and played sounds. He patented his first invention as an adult. But inventors can be any age and from anywhere. Did you know that trampolines and popsicles are children's inventions? An invention by a child even led to the invention of the technology inside your TV!

Inventors look for ways to improve people's lives. They identify a problem, then make something to solve it. Their invention could be an object or just a new way of doing something. Often, inventions make the world a better place. Let's look at two examples …

Elif Bilgin, from Turkey, is a young inventor. She was 16 when she invented a process that turns banana skins into plastic. She worked on it for more than two years. She won Google's Science in Action award because her invention could reduce pollution.

Hal Abelson is an older inventor. He started working as a computer scientist over 40 years ago. He is part of a team that developed AppInventor—software that makes it easy for people to program their own apps for mobile devices. It helps people all over the world, including children in poor countries, to make apps. These apps can improve communities, for example, by helping people to collect water, clean up trash, and even detect fires.

Could you be an inventor? Well, to be a good inventor, you have to think creatively about solving problems—connecting different ideas and experimenting with different methods and materials. You also need to be able to talk to and listen to the people who might use your invention. But it's important to keep trying when your ideas don't work out. Do you have these skills? If so, what are you waiting for?

3 Write the main ideas in the correct order.

> An example of an older inventor   Inventors try to make people's lives better
>
> Inventors are of any age   The qualities of a good inventor
>
> An example of a younger inventor

Paragraph 1 _____

Paragraph 2 _____

Paragraph 3 _____

Paragraph 4 _____

Paragraph 5 _____

4 Match the details below to paragraphs above. Write a number.

a Her invention turns banana skins into plastic. ☐

b If something doesn't work, you should try again. ☐

c An invention can be an object or a process. ☐

d You can use his invention on a smartphone. ☐

e Edison invented some things we use every day. ☐

5 Write one more detail from each paragraph.

Paragraph 1 _____

_____

Paragraph 2 _____

_____

Paragraph 3 _____

_____

Paragraph 4 _____

_____

Paragraph 5 _____

Present Perfect Questions (*yes/no*)

Have **you** heard **of Thomas Edison?** Yes, **I** have. / **No, I** haven't.
Have **we** been **here before?** Yes, **we** have. / **No, we** haven't.
Have **they ever** built **a robot?** Yes, **they** have. / **No, they** haven't.

1 **Complete the sentences from the song on page 56 of the Student's Book.**

  a Have you ever _____ to Jupiter? (be)

  b Have you ever _____ an X-ray? (have)

  c Have you ever _____ a new invention? (make)

  d Have you ever _____ a car? (drive)

2 **Circle.**

  a **Have / Has** you ever spoken to a robot?

  b **Have / Has** he ever developed an app?

  c **Have / Has** they ever visited us?

  d Have you ever broken your screen? No, I **haven't / didn't**.

  e Have you ever been to South America? Yes, I **went / have**.

  f Have you ever invented anything? Yes, **I have / did**.

3 **Complete with the present perfect.**

a _____ you ever _____ (be) on TV?

b _____ you ever _____ (cook) spaghetti?

c _____ you ever _____ (see) a shark?

d _____ he ever _____ (climb) a tree?

e _____ we ever _____ (eat) octopus?

f _____ they ever _____ (build) a house?

4 **Write and answer questions with the present perfect and *ever*.**

_____ she
_____
_____
(fly / on a plane)?
✓ _____
_____

_____ he
_____
_____
(swim / in the ocean)?
✗ _____
_____

_____ they
_____
_____
(go / into the jungle)?
✓ _____
_____

_____ they
_____
_____
(win / a tournament)?
✗ _____
_____

My Life

Write three questions with *Have you ever ... ?* Then, answer for you.

a see / a drone _____

_____

b have / a smartphone _____

_____

c take / a selfie _____

_____

1 Say and write the words. Underline *ow*, *oa*, or *oe*.

_ _ _ _ _ _ _

_ _ _ _ _ _ _

_ _ _ _ _ _ _

_ _ _ _ _ _ _

_ _ _ _ _ _ _

_ _ _ _ _ _ _

2 Circle the word with the different vowel sound.

a snow   how   throw   d coat   town   toe

b allow   blow   slow   e road   oboe   flower

c grow   goat   cow   f show   shoe   throw

Oracy

1 Answer the questions.

a What was the name of your group's invention and one of its special features?

_____

b What was the name of another group's invention and one of its special features?

_____

c What questions did you ask to check understanding?

_____

d What questions did you ask to get further information?

_____

Prepositions Following Adjectives

Some adjectives are followed by a preposition, such as *about*, *with*, or *at*. There isn't a special pattern to these—you just need to learn them!

| **be** excited about | **be** pleased with | **be** terrible at | **be** interested in |
| **be** married to | **be** proud of | **be** responsible for | **be** different from |

1. **Read and circle.**

   a Evie was proud **of** / **with** herself for winning the science competition.

   b Charles Babbage is famous **about** / **for** inventing the first computer.

   c Mom was angry **with** / **about** me when I broke her phone!

   d The teacher was surprised **with** / **at** all our ideas.

   e My friends and I are interested **in** / **on** computer animation.

2. **Complete.**

   with   of   at   to   about

   a My Uncle Tom is married _____ my Aunt Sarah.

   b Lucy was feeling anxious _____ the test.

   c Are you scared _____ the dark?

   d I was really happy _____ the photos I took on my phone.

   e The children were not good _____ math!

3. **Read and complete with the correct prepositions.**

   Grace Hopper was a mathematician and computer scientist. She is famous I _____ inventing early computer languages like COBOL. She was born in New York in 1906. As a child, she was very curious 2 _____ machines. She was very good 3 _____ taking clocks apart. After studying math in college, she became interested 4 _____ computers. She joined a research team at Harvard University and then worked at a technology company. She was responsible 5 _____ creating a new way of programming computers using language. It was different 6 _____ the old way, which used a code of numbers.

1 **READ** **Answer the question.**

How did Shamsa feel about some of the inventions? _____

From: shamsa457@kidsworld.com   **To:** babu100@kidsworld.com   **Subject:** Awesome day at the tech fair!

Hi Babu,

How was your weekend?

Today I went to a technology fair in my city—it was so cool! There was lots of new technology. I was really surprised at some of the inventions. The craziest thing was seeing robots that talk and do other activities, too, like play the piano and play games like chess. I'd love to have a robot in my house! The coolest thing I saw was a pair of high-tech sneakers that change color when you press a button on your smartphone!

We learned all about electronics and even took a look inside a computer.

You should come to the fair with me next year. I know you are curious about all the new inventions coming out.

I'll attach a photo I took. I'm really happy with it.

Take care,

Shamsa

2 **PLAN** **Prepare to write an email about technology. Complete the graphic organizer.**

- A trip to the science museum
- An amazing piece of technology I have seen

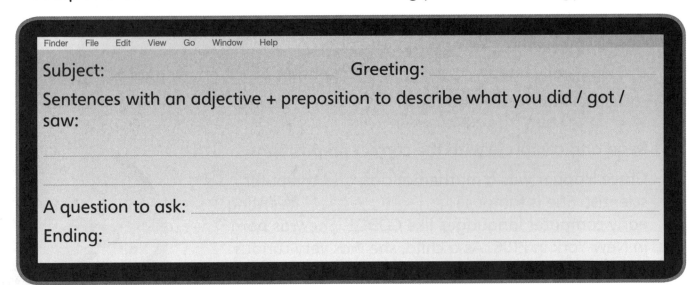

Finder   File   Edit   View   Go   Window   Help

Subject: _____   Greeting: _____

Sentences with an adjective + preposition to describe what you did / got / saw:

_____

_____

A question to ask: _____

Ending: _____

3 **WRITE** **Use the graphic organizer to write your email in your notebooks.**

4 **EDIT** **Did you ...**

☐ include a subject?   ☐ include a greeting and an ending?

☐ include a question?   ☐ use prepositions with adjectives correctly?

1 Key Words 4 **Which word can't be used? Cross it out.**

1 The robot's _____ looked very real.

   a memory **b** eyebrows **c** facial expressions

2 The robot sounded like a _____.

   a human being **b** female **c** owner

3 Someone's _____ can tell you what they are thinking.

   a facial expressions **b** human being **c** body language

4 The robot's voice sounded _____.

   a puzzled **b** natural **c** facial

5 Anna wasn't sure how to _____ when the robot spoke.

   a allow **b** react **c** answer

2 **Complete.**

> female owner natural puzzled memory react

a Tom didn't know how to _____ to the news.

b The dog always sat when its _____ said "Sit!"

c My new computer has lots of _____—it's very powerful.

d Do you think robots can be male or _____, or are they always "it"?

e I love _____ materials, like wood and stone.

f Did you understand what the teacher said? You look a bit _____.

1 **Look and answer. Do you think the girl likes the robot?**

2 **Read. Underline the main ideas in paragraphs I and 2.**

Reading Strategy: Identifying the Main Idea and Details

Remember, the main idea of a paragraph is normally supported by details. Often, the main idea can be found in the first sentence.

What Was It Thinking?

Luisa was puzzled. She looked at its shiny metal suspiciously. Its face looked almost human—it even had eyebrows. But what, if anything, was it thinking? Luisa wasn't sure that she could trust it, because its facial expression wasn't completely natural. And then there was the mystery of her missing clothes …

Luisa's parents were very pleased with the HELPA—or Humanoid Everyday Living Personal Assistant. They bought it to help them keep the house cleaner and neater. It whizzed quietly around the house, washing, wiping, cleaning, and picking up. Within seconds of the family's finishing a meal, the HELPA took away the plates and knives and forks and washed them. If Luisa or her brother spilled any food, the HELPA cleaned it up right away. And no one tripped on things on the stairs anymore. But still, Luisa wasn't sure about it.

"Mom, I think there's a problem with the HELPA."

"Really?" her mom replied. "But don't you remember how the house used to be so messy? It wasn't as clean and neat as this before!"

"But I can't find three of my T-shirts or my favorite socks. Maybe there's a problem with its memory, or we made a mistake when we programmed it. Or else it's just hiding my stuff!"

Just then, the HELPA stopped suddenly as it whizzed past them.

"Your T-shirts and socks are in the trash can," it said, in a nearly-but-not-quite-human voice. "I wash dirty clothes from the laundry basket and put away clean clothes in drawers. I do not have a program for dirty clothes on the floor."

Luisa's mom laughed. "Well, what a clever machine! I think we'll keep you programmed that way!"

3 Read again and circle the best summary—*a*, *b*, or *c*.

a Paragraph 1   Luisa was very happy with the robot.

Paragraph 2   Luisa's parents were very happy with the robot.

b Paragraph 1   Luisa was not very happy with the robot.

Paragraph 2   Luisa's parents were not very happy with the robot.

c Paragraph 1   Luisa was not very happy with the robot.

Paragraph 2   Luisa's parents were very happy with the robot.

4 Which paragraph do the details appear in? Read and write *1* or *2*.

a The HELPA has some human features on its face. _____

b The HELPA does the dishes after meals. _____

c Some of Luisa's clothes have disappeared. _____

d The HELPA works quickly. _____

e The HELPA cleans and picks up. _____

f The HELPA is made of metal. _____

5 Read and circle *T* (true) or *F* (false).

a The house was cleaner before than it is now.   T   F

b Luisa can't find her favorite socks.   T   F

c The HELPA's voice sounds very human.   T   F

d There is a problem with the HELPA's memory.   T   F

e Luisa's mom thinks what the HELPA did was funny. T   F

6 What do you think is the main message of the story? Mark ✓.

a The HELPA wanted to hide Luisa's clothes. ☐

b Luisa should put her dirty clothes in the laundry basket. ☐

c Luisa should wash her own clothes. ☐

7 What do you do to help keep your home neat?

_____

_____

_____

Grammar in Context

Used to / didn't use to

I **used to** **watch different TV programs.**
The house **used to** **be so messy.**
My cousins **used to** **live in a different city.**
I **didn't use to** **have a smartphone.**

Sam **didn't use to** **play computer games when he was younger.**
My parents **didn't use to** **have the Internet at home.**
Did you **use to** **ride your bike to school?**
Yes, I did. **/ No, I** didn't.

1 Match.

1 They used to eat a lot of junk food,
2 I used to go to bed very late,
3 He didn't use to speak English,
4 You used to be shy,
5 We didn't use to live in this town,
6 They didn't use to like each other,

a but now you're much more confident.
b but now they're good friends.
c but now I go earlier.
d but now they eat healthier food.
e but now he has learned a lot.
f but we moved when I was three.

2 Look at the pictures from the past and complete with *used to* or *didn't use to*.

We _____ go on vacation to the beach.

She _____ have short hair.

They _____ live in the city.

I _____ love ice cream!

3 Write sentences with *used to* ✓ / *didn't use to* ✗.

a we / live / in an apartment ✓

_____

b Eva / like / spicy food ✗

_____

c cell phones / be / much bigger ✓

_____

d I / take / selfies ✗

_____

e My parents / go / to an Internet café to send emails ✓

_____

f Grandpa / have / a smartphone ✗

_____

4 Make questions with *use to*.

When you were six, ….

a you / enjoy school?

_____ ?

_____

b you / play / any sports?

_____ ?

_____

c you / have / a pet?

_____ ?

_____

d you / walk to school?

_____ ?

_____

5 Write short answers to the questions in Activity 4.

6 Read and answer. Write full sentences.

a Which TV programs did you use to watch most when you were younger?

_____

b Which toys did you use to play with when you were five?

_____

c Write one thing that you didn't use to like but you like now.

_____

1 What do you know about using the Internet safely? Complete the rules for staying safe on the Internet with *Do* or *Don't*.

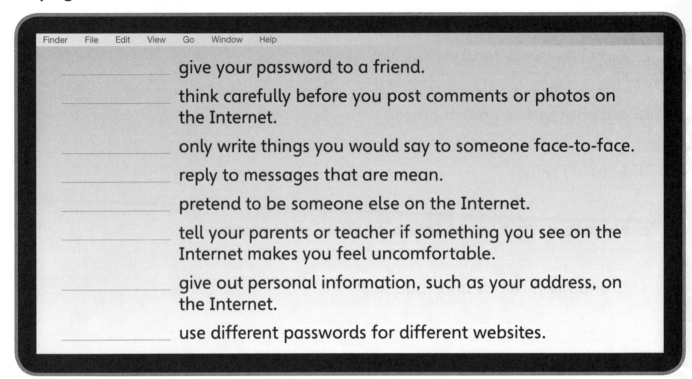

Finder   File   Edit   View   Go   Window   Help

_____ give your password to a friend.

_____ think carefully before you post comments or photos on the Internet.

_____ only write things you would say to someone face-to-face.

_____ reply to messages that are mean.

_____ pretend to be someone else on the Internet.

_____ tell your parents or teacher if something you see on the Internet makes you feel uncomfortable.

_____ give out personal information, such as your address, on the Internet.

_____ use different passwords for different websites.

2 Who is using the Internet safely? Look and mark ✓.

3 Why is using the Internet safely important?

_____

_____

_____

Check Your Oracy!

1 I asked questions to check understanding.   **Yes / No**

2 I asked questions to get more information. **Yes / No**

The Big Challenge

How can we imagine the world in 10 years' time?

1 **Color the stars to give yourself a score.***

I thought of some ideas and shared them with my group.	☆☆☆☆☆
I helped to draw and label our poster.	☆☆☆☆☆
I practiced presenting our poster with my group.	☆☆☆☆☆
I presented our poster with my group.	☆☆☆☆☆
I asked questions about the other presentations.	☆☆☆☆☆

*(5 = Awesome! 4 = Pretty good, 3 = OK, 2 = Could be better, 1 = Needs more work!)

2 **Which idea did you like best?**

_____

3 **Which change do you think will happen first?**

_____

The Big Question and Me

Because of the things I have learned in this unit,

1 I will _____ .

2 I will _____ .

SB page 69

1 **Circle.**

   a Which **search engine** / **screen** did you use to find the information you needed?

   b **Internet** / **Technology** might make transportation faster and safer.

   c Oh, no! The **screen** / **invention** of my phone is broken.

   d A tablet is a kind of **search engine** / **mobile device**.

   e Do your parents **connect** / **allow** you to have your own phone?

   f Oh, no! I can't **allow** / **connect** to the Internet!

2 **Complete.**

> program   software   selfie   animation   manufacturers   apps

   a I love that _____ of you and your sister. Where did you take it?

   b You can get thousands of useful _____ for your phone.

   c My brother taught himself to _____ a computer.

   d Some car _____ are making driverless cars.

   e Do you have the newest version of this computer _____?

   f There's a lot of _____ in the movie.

3 **Complete.**

> natural   expressions   female
> human being   puzzled   body language

When I look at my old toy robot in the corner of my room, I feel I 1 _____. I don't play with it much now, but I don't want to throw it away. I'm not sure why. It doesn't really look like a 2 _____. It doesn't have human facial 3 _____ or use human 4 _____. It isn't male or 5 _____, and it doesn't look very 6 _____. But I can't help thinking it's a little bit human …

3

4 **Complete with the present perfect.**

a _____ you ever _____ (use) a search engine?

b _____ you ever _____ (see) a drone?

c _____ your parents ever _____ (allow) you to stay up past midnight?

d _____ he ever _____ (make) an animation? No, he _____.

e _____ she ever _____ (program) a computer? Yes, she _____.

f _____ we ever _____ (write) an app? No, we _____.

5 **Write sentences about Eric with *used to / didn't use to*.**

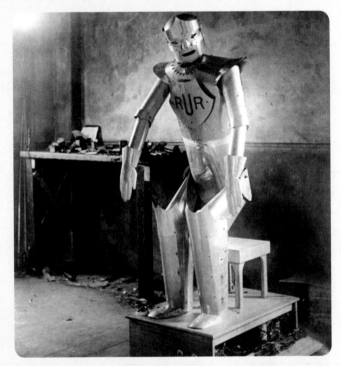

> This is Eric. He's my robot. He could sit, stand, and talk, but he couldn't walk or move his fingers. He can't do those things anymore. He's broken.

✓	✗
sit	walk
stand	move his fingers
talk	

Eric _____ .

He _____ .

_____

_____

6 **Read and complete with a preposition.**

a Steve Jobs is famous _____ co-founding Apple.

b Are you excited _____ getting a new smartphone?

c I'm interested _____ apps that can create animations from images.

1 **Read and answer.**

a How many functions did your group think of in total? _____

b Which four functions did you choose?

_____

_____

_____

_____

c Which function did you think was best?

_____

2 **What are the speakers doing? Write *a*, *b*, *c*, or *d*.**

a Asking a question to get clarity.

b Recognizing and respecting a classmate's opinion.

c Setting ground rules for a discussion.

d Asking a question to get further information.

1 I think that we shouldn't talk over each other.　　I agree. _____

2 Where does the word *robot* come from?　　A science fiction writer first used the word *robot* in a play in 1920. _____

3 *Robot* is a Czech word.　　Can you repeat that? _____

4 Anyway, I think the robot should do our homework.　　That's a good point, but how would we learn anything? _____

3 **What did you say? Write an example.**

a recognizing and respecting your classmates' opinions

_____

b asking a question to find out more information

_____

c asking a question to check you understood

_____

What can you remember about ... Unit 3?

1 Circle.

Can you help me **allow / join / connect** to the Internet?

2 What is this part of a mobile device called?

_____

3 What is this? Mark ✓.

a search engine ☐
a drone ☐
an animation ☐

4 Complete.

We can p_____ computers to make them do many different tasks.

5 How does ELSA's owner look? Circle.

nervous
embarrassed
puzzled

6 What is this? _____

7 Complete and answer for you.

Have you ever _____ (live) without technology for a week? _____

8 Complete. Use *used to / didn't use to*.

ELSA's voice _____ sound boring. It _____ sound very "human" or natural.

Read and complete with a preposition.

9 Shamsa was really surprised _____ some of the inventions at the tech fair.

10 She was really happy _____ the photos she took.

Check your answers in the Student's Book. How did you do?

10 ☐ Wow! 8–9 ☐ Great! 6–7 ☐ Good! 0–5 ☐ Try harder!

? 😀 **Is technology good or bad?** Write your answer to the Big Question.

_____
_____
_____

How do we entertain ourselves?

1 ▶ 4.1 **Watch the video. Complete the graphic organizer.**

> art   running   music   soccer   dancing   swimming
> basketball   craft activities   cycling   drama

Sports on Our Own	Leisure Activities	Creative Activities
	Team Sports	

2 Key Words 1 **Complete.**

> drama   collect   play   imagination   origami   rehearsing   leisure   craft

Olly and Kimi both like creative activities. You have
to use your 1 _____ for these activities.

I'm crazy about 2 _____ ! I always want
to be in the school 3 _____ . I spend
a lot of my free time learning the words and
4 _____ .

OLLY

KIMI

I love making things with my hands. I really like
5 _____ activities. I 6 _____
nice pieces of paper. I do 7 _____ .
One of my favorite 8 _____ activities is
making paper animals.

1 Key Words 2 **Match.**

1 blog
2 board game
3 vlog
4 post
5 upload
6 link
7 click

a to move information from one device to another
b the address of another website
c a website where you write about your interests
d a website with video where you talk about your interests
e to select text and press a computer key or mouse
f a piece of writing on a blog
g something you can play with friends—not on a computer

2 **Circle.**

a The difference between a blog and a vlog is that a **blog / vlog** has video.

b I love writing about music and movies, so I started writing a **blog / vlog**.

c Have you read my latest blog **post / link**?

d I'm trying to **upload / click** these photos to my blog.

e I don't like staring at a screen—I prefer to play **video games / board games**.

f Can you send me the **link / post** to the website about origami?

g Can you help? Nothing happens when I **upload / click** on the button.

3 **Complete.**

    links   click   post   upload   blog

How to Plan and Design a Blog

• First, choose a name for your 1 _____.

• Then, choose photos, text styles, and colors to match your personality!

• Start writing your first 2 _____.

• Read and re-read what you've written. 3 _____ photos and 4 _____.

• When you are ready, 5 _____ Save!

(1) **Look. What kind of games is the blog about? Circle.**

   a outdoor games   b board games   c video games

Reading Strategy: Annotating: *what, how, where, why, who*

Underlining important information in texts can help us understand them. Finding answers to simple questions with *what*, *how*, *where*, *why*, and *who* helps identify essential information.

HOME | BLOG

Welcome to the Games Club Blog!

The Games Club meets every Thursday, from 3:00 to 4:30, in the fifth-grade classroom. The main aim is to have fun playing board games. We play old games that I loved when I was a child, new games that members are excited to try, and games from all over the world!

Next Week

Did you know that some board games are over 5,000 years old? Next week, we'll take a look at one of the oldest—Go. Have you ever played it? It's one of my favorites.

It's for two players, and it's very simple to play. You start with an empty board. If you're just starting to play, you can play with a board that's nine lines by nine lines. Then, you need "stones." One person has black stones, and the other has white stones. You take turns putting a stone on the board. The aim of the game is to put stones around empty spaces to make "territories" (areas) or to put stones around the other player's stones to "capture" them.

I like it because the rules are simple, but the game can be very complex. It can change very quickly, and surprising things can happen.

If you want to check out some more facts about Go, click on this <u>link</u>.

Can you find out where Go is from? If you know, post a comment below.

Comment

Hello! I'm Mrs. Maxwell, and I run the Games Club (and I teach fifth grade!). My interests are music, camping, and playing board games. My perfect day is walking in the countryside, singing around a campfire, and playing a board game with friends—ideally, with a big mug of hot chocolate!

2 **Read the blog. Then, underline the answers to the questions.**

a Where does Games Club meet?

b Who is writing the blog?

c What is the writer's favorite board game?

d How do you play the game?

e Why does the writer like the game?

3 **Match the answers below to the questions above. Write a letter *a–e*.**

1 Go _____

2 You start with an empty board ... _____

3 Mrs. Maxwell _____

4 In the fifth grade classroom _____

5 The rules are simple but the game can be very complex. _____

4 **Read and circle *T* (true) or *F* (false).**

a Games Club meets once a week.   T   F

b You can only play old games at Games Club.   T   F

c They played Go last week at Games Club.   T   F

d The rules of Go are easy to understand.   T   F

e Mrs. Maxwell is a teacher.   T   F

f Mrs. Maxwell doesn't like outdoor activities.   T   F

5 **Read and answer.**

a Have you heard of Go? _____

b Have you ever played Go? _____

c What's your favorite board game? Why do you like it?

_____

_____

Grammar in Context

Present Perfect with *ever* and *never*

Have **you** ever played **Go?**	**I**'ve never done **origami.**
Has **it** ever snowed **on your birthday?**	**Dad** has never posted **a comment on a blog.**
Have **they** ever acted **in a play?**	**We**'ve never been **camping.**

1 Complete the sentences from the song on page 78 of the Student's Book.

a I've never _____ insects. (eat)

b I've never _____ with sharks. (swim)

c I've never _____ banana juice. (drink)

d I've never _____ skateboarding in the park. (be)

e I've never _____ online. (chat)

f I've never _____ the Internet. (use)

2 Complete with *ever* or *never*.

a Have you _____ met a famous person?

b My grandpa has _____ been to a foreign country.

c Our cousins have _____ stayed with us before.

d Has he _____ baked a cake?

e I've _____ been to Australia.

f Have they _____ slept under the stars?

3 Write the words in the right order to make questions and sentences.

a online / ever / written / you / something / Have / ?

_____

b have / an / app / I / made / never

_____

c rained / in / Has / the / ever / desert / it / ?

_____

d never / bike / has / a / She / ridden

_____

4 Read. Write questions with the present perfect and *ever*.

This is Tim Berners-Lee. He is a British computer scientist. He invented the World Wide Web. The first web page appeared online in 1991.

a study / in college?

_____

_____

Yes, he has. He studied physics at Oxford University.

b work / in a foreign country?

_____

Yes, he has. He was working at a physics laboratory in Switzerland when he invented the World Wide Web.

c have / any interests apart from computers?

_____

Yes, he has. When he was a child, he loved playing with model trains.

My Life

Write three things you have never done.

a I have never _____ .

b I _____ .

c _____

1 **Say and write the words. Underline** *ue*, *ew*, **or** *oo*.

_____

_____

_____

_____

_____

_____

2 **Circle the word with the different vowel sound.**

a blue   book   blew   c knew   moon   wood   e few   too   look

b good   glue   grew   d statue   flood   Sue   f foot   food   boot

Oracy

1 **Read.**

a Mark a phrase that expresses an opinion.

b Circle a phrase that shows someone agrees.

c Underline a phrase that shows someone disagrees.

Liam So … What's your favorite thing to do after school?

Kate Good question, Liam. The school day is so long! I always need to rest my brain before I do my homework. I love watching videos online. I think it's very relaxing.

Jack Watching videos after school? Really? I disagree, because it's boring to be inside on a computer after sitting in school all day. I love going outside and skateboarding. I think getting some exercise is better for your brain and your body.

Liam I agree, because I love being outside, too. Cycling is awesome, and I'm crazy about surfing when it's a sunny day. I really get tired of being on a computer all the time.

Also, too, either

We use *also* and *too* to add extra information after a positive verb. *Too* is more common than *also* in informal contexts. *Too* and *also* go in different positions in a sentence.

Too usually goes at the end of a sentence.

I love drama, and I love dancing, too.

Also usually goes just before the verb.

I love drama, and I also **love dancing.**

Also goes after the verb *to be* and modal verbs.

They are friendly, and they are also **funny.**

They can also **speak Turkish.**

In verbs with two parts, *also* goes between the first and second parts.

I have also **been to the jungle.**

We are also **going to Mexico.**

We use *either* after a negative verb.

He doesn't like camping, and he doesn't like hiking either.

1) **Read and circle.**

a I can speak English. I can **too / also** speak Spanish.

b I didn't like the movie **also / either**.

c Carla loves cycling, and Ana loves it, **too / either**.

d We are tired, and we are **too / also** hungry.

e My friends don't want to go swimming. I don't want to go swimming **either / also**.

f Are they coming to the beach with us, **either / too**?

2) **Complete with *also*, *too*, or *either*.**

a Tim loves trampolining. He _____ likes gymnastics.

b I don't like tomatoes. I don't like cheese _____ .

c Would you like to come camping, _____?

d We've been to South America. We've _____ been to Europe.

e She forgot her boots. She didn't remember the ball _____!

f I enjoy painting. I really enjoy craft activities, _____ .

g Wow! You can play the piano, and you can _____ play the violin.

h My grandparents are kind. They are _____ funny.

1 READ Answer the question.

What did Tomoko's favorite player give her? _____

Tomoko's Soccer Adventures

Welcome to my world of soccer!

SUNDAY, NOVEMBER 26

Today was incredible! Dad took me to watch the best soccer team ever! I was really excited to watch my favorite team.

"Come on, Reds!" we cheered.

I was wearing my team T-shirt, and Dad also had his team scarf on. When the game started, the boys next to me started singing—I joined in, too!

Our team played really well, but they didn't score in the first half, or the second half, either. I was pretty disappointed, but after the game, something amazing happened! We were in the parking lot, and suddenly we saw my favorite soccer player,

the goalkeeper for the Reds. Then, guess what? I told him I was a fan, and he gave me a professional soccer ball and signed it!

I'm going to be watching the next game on December 10th on TV. Maybe we'll have better luck then.

2 PLAN Prepare to write a blog post about one of your interests and something that happened. Complete the graphic organizer.

Interest
_____

Day and Date
_____

What happened?
_____
_____
_____
_____

How did you feel?
What did you think?
_____
_____
_____
_____
_____

About me!
_____
_____
_____
_____

3 WRITE Use the graphic organizer to write and design your blog post in your notebooks.

4 EDIT Did you ...

☐ include the day and date?

☐ write in the first person?

☐ include your opinions?

☐ use also, too, and either correctly?

1 Key Words 4 Complete.

lonely   distracted   behavior   whisper   surroundings
move   pay attention   comforting

a Shhh! If you need to talk in the library, please _____.

b Did you feel _____ on your first day at your new school?

c I love the smell of toast—I find it really _____.

d The teacher asked the class to _____ and listen carefully.

e I couldn't focus on my work last night—I was _____ by the soccer game on TV.

f Paula's family will _____ if her mom gets a new job.

g It can take time to feel comfortable in new _____.

h Sometimes, our teacher gives us extra play time for good _____.

2 Find the words!

behavior   comforting
excitement   distracted
move   pay attention
lonely   shake hands
surroundings   whisper

L	C	R	L	D	Y	Y	A	I	C	S	N
Y	O	U	O	L	M	O	T	O	F	U	O
M	M	N	Q	I	O	V	M	Q	M	R	I
K	O	T	E	Z	V	F	I	K	D	R	T
Q	V	C	C	L	O	A	N	P	D	O	N
J	E	U	R	R	Y	L	H	H	Q	U	E
D	I	S	T	R	A	C	T	E	D	N	T
W	H	I	S	P	E	R	O	A	B	D	T
T	N	E	M	E	T	I	C	X	E	I	A
G	Y	S	N	P	G	W	W	J	R	N	Y
S	D	N	A	H	E	K	A	H	S	G	A
T	C	G	M	H	Z	G	R	F	B	S	P

1) **Look. What information does the picture give you about the characters and the setting?**

Characters: _____

Setting: _____

2) **Read. Can you add anything to your ideas in Activity 1? Do you need to change anything?**

Reading Strategy: Identifying Plot, Character, and Setting

The plot means the events of the story. The characters are the people in the story. The setting means the place where it happens.

A Dramatic New Start!

"My dad got a new job," said Sarah, without much excitement.

"That's good, isn't it?" asked Sophie.

"Well … kind of. It means we have to move."

"But you're always saying your house is too small, right?"

"Yes … "

"And maybe you'll get your own room."

"Soph, please stop talking for a minute, and pay attention! We're moving to Cardiff, in Wales—it's 200 miles away!"

"Oh," Sophie stopped suddenly.

Sarah and Sophie met on their first day at pre-school. They were great friends from that day on, but they were very different. Sophie loved sports and was always running around, full of energy. If she wasn't doing gymnastics, she was swimming or maybe doing judo. Sarah was quieter. She loved reading and doing craft activities, too. The big interest that they shared was drama.

"Have you found a new house yet?" asked Sophie quietly.

"Not yet, but Mom and Dad are looking. And they've already visited two schools. But I won't have any friends when I start school there. I hope I won't feel too lonely."

The two girls sat in silence for a while. Sophie looked around at the comforting surroundings of Sarah's room—the shelves of books, the colorful drawings, and the class photos from every year of school. And the posters from school plays with their names on them.

"I have an idea," Sophie announced.

"Hmmmm?"

"Did you say Cardiff? My cousin lives in Cardiff, and he's in a drama club there. He loves it!"

"Really?"

"Yes! I could give you my aunt's phone number. Then, your mom could call his mom when you get there, and maybe you could go along and try it out. I could come and visit you there, too."

"That would be amazing! Thanks, Sophie— you're a real friend."

3 Which character do you think is most likely to say each phrase? Write it in the correct place.

- I went for a run.

- Have you read this book?

- Do you want to come swimming with me?

- Let's rehearse our words for the play!

- I'm making a birthday card out of flowers.

Sophie   Sarah

_____   _____
                _____
_____   _____

4 Which of these sentences are about the plot? Which are about the characters? Which are about the setting? Write *P*, *C*, or *S*.

a Sophie loved sports and was always running around, full of energy. _____

b Sophie looked around at the comforting surroundings of Sarah's room. _____

c "Well … kind of. It means we have to move." _____

d And the posters from school plays with their names on them. _____

e Sarah was quieter. _____

f "I hope I won't feel too lonely." _____

5 Read again and circle the best summary—*a*, *b* or *c*.

a Sarah has to move to another city. She is looking forward to making new friends and starting new hobbies in her new city.

b Sarah has to move to another city. She is worried that she will be lonely. Her friend tells her about someone with the same hobby in her new city.

c Sarah has to move to another city. She is worried that she will be lonely. Her friend says she should try a new hobby in her new city.

Present Perfect with *already*, *just*, **and** *yet*

We've just moved **to this neighborhood.**
"Have you found **a new house** yet?"
"No, not yet."

It hasn't snowed yet **this winter.**
He's already eaten, **so he isn't hungry.**
They've already visited **two schools.**

1 **Circle.**

a This book was so easy to read—I've finished it **just / already**.

b He hasn't started his homework **yet / already**.

c They've **just / yet** finished their test, so they're very happy.

d Have you sent that email **yet / just**?

e We don't know anyone—we've **just / already** moved here.

f My project is going really well—I've **already / just** done most of it.

2 **What has just happened? Complete with** *just* **and the present perfect.**

He _____
(fall) off his bike.

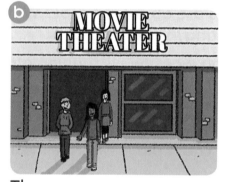

They _____
(see) a movie.

She _____
(upload) some photos.

They _____
(made) some origami
animals.

It _____
(rain).

We _____
(clean) the car.

3 **Complete with *just*, *yet*, or *already*.**

a We've _____ been to that campsite. We went last year.

b They haven't finished their art project _____ .

c Oh, no! I've _____ dropped the paint!

d He doesn't want to see that movie again. He's _____ seen it twice.

e Have you learned your words for the play _____ ?

f Look! I've _____ written my first blog post.

4 **Read and write.**

This is TechStar Tess.
It's 12:25 on Wednesday.

Wednesday		
9:00	Write blog	✓
10:00	Work on new animation	✓
11:00	Design an app	✓
12:30	Lunch	

To Do

upload selfies

wash the drone

a What has TechStar Tess already done today? Write two things.

_____

_____

b What has she just done?

_____

c What has she not done yet? Write three things.

_____

_____

_____

5 **Read and write. Use the present perfect.**

a Write two things you've already done this year.

I've already _____.

I _____.

b Write two things you've just done.

I've just _____.

I _____.

c Write two things you haven't done yet this week.

I haven't _____.

_____.

1 **Look and complete.**

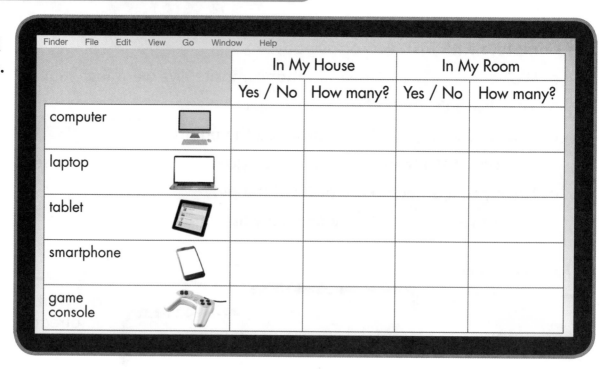

Finder File Edit View Go Window Help	In My House		In My Room	
	Yes / No	How many?	Yes / No	How many?
computer				
laptop				
tablet				
smartphone				
game console				

2 **How many hours of screen time do you have each week? Circle.**

less than 7   7–14   14–21   21–28   more than 28

3 **What do you think can be some of the disadvantages of a lot of screen time? Look and circle.**

a You could become more **tired** / **healthy** and less **tired** / **healthy**.

b You could feel more **nervous** / **confident** and **anxious** / **happy** if you spend less time with people.

c You might have **more** / **fewer** friends because you don't have time to see them.

d You might be **more** / **less** distracted at school if you go to bed too late.

4 **Who is trying to reduce their screen time? Look and mark ✓.**

5 **Why is reducing screen time in our free time important?**

_____

_____

Check Your Oracy!

1 I listened to the opinions of the other people in my group. **Yes / No**

2 I gave reasons for agreeing or disagreeing. **Yes / No**

3 I used the phrases on the cue cards. **Yes / No**

The Big Challenge

How can we make entertainment?

1 **Color the stars to give yourself a score.***

I thought of lots of ideas for my character.	☆☆☆☆☆
I drew and labeled my character.	☆☆☆☆☆
I practiced presenting my character to my group.	☆☆☆☆☆
I presented my character to my group.	☆☆☆☆☆
I listened to the other character ideas in my group.	☆☆☆☆☆

*(5 = Awesome! 4 = Pretty good, 3 = OK, 2 = Could be better, I = Needs more work!)

2 **Which cartoon character idea did you like best? Why?**

_____

_____

The Big Question and **Me**

Because of the things I have learned in this unit,

1 I will _____.

2 I will _____.

1 **Circle.**

1 Sports, drama, and camping are all _____ activities.

   a craft   **b** origami   **c** leisure

2 Creative activites involve using our _____ .

   a drama   **b** leisure   **c** imaginations

3 Come on! It's time to _____ the play.

   a rehearse   **b** collect   **c** display

4 I like making things, so I do a lot of _____ activities.

   a drama   **b** craft   **c** imagination

5 _____ is his passion. He always wants to be in the school play!

   a Origami   **b** Drama   **c** Leisure

2 **Complete.**

links
post
click
blog
designs
vlog
upload

Finder   File   Edit   View   Go   Window   Help

Hi, I'm Em. I'm crazy about building things, so I decided to start a
1 _____ about it. At the moment, I write a new 2 _____ every week. I 3 _____ photos of my 4 _____ .
I also include 5 _____ to websites with more ideas for building. If I can get my friend to video me, I'll make it into a 6 _____ . Then, I can show you exactly how I build things. Do you want to read my blog? Just 7 _____ here ...

GO TO EM'S BLOG

3 **Read and circle.**

a Hot food can be very **lonely** / **comforting** on a cold day.

b Pay attention! Try not to get so **comforting** / **distracted** when you're studying!

c The house was in beautiful **surroundings** / **behavior**.

d What's all the **excitement** / **surroundings** about?

e Mom **whispered** / **paid attention** quietly in my ear.

f I'm not happy about your **excitement** / **behavior**.

4 **Make sentences and questions with *ever* or *never* and the present perfect.**

a _____ you _____ (collect) anything as a hobby?

b I _____ (climb) a mountain.

c My dad _____ (act) in a play.

d _____ they _____ (swim) in the sea?

e We _____ (go) camping in winter.

f _____ he _____ (invent) a board game?

5 **Complete with *just*, *yet*, or *already*.**

a Mom is tired. She's _____ arrived home from work.

b I'm hungry! I haven't had breakfast _____.

c They've _____ finished their homework. That was quick!

d Have you played your new board game _____?

e I've _____ seen a really funny cartoon!

f We've _____ rehearsed the play five times. It's going to be great!

6 **What does Freddie like? Make sentences with (*not*) *like* and *also*, *too*, or *either*.**

✓
cycling
soccer
drama
board games

✗
craft activities
relaxing

a He _____ cycling, and he _____ soccer, _____.

b He _____ drama, and he _____ _____ board games.

c He _____ craft activities, and he _____ relaxing _____!

SPEAKING MISSION

1 **What did they say? Complete the conversations.**

> instrument   music stand   balcony   concert   mandolin   stage

Kalil Did you have a good weekend?

Akira It was pretty good.

Kalil What did you do?

Akira I played in a 1 _____.

Kalil Really? I didn't know you played an 2 _____!

Akira Yeah, I play the 3 _____.

Kalil That's awesome! Where did you play?

Akira At the National Theater.

Kalil Really? That's so cool. Who did you go with?

Akira My parents. They always come to my concerts. They watched me from the 4 _____.

Kalil What did you wear?

Akira I wore a long black dress with black shoes.

Kalil What did you take with you?

Akira Just my mandolin, a 5 _____, and sheet music!

Kalil Did you get nervous when you went on 6 _____?

Akira Yes, of course! I always get nervous. But when I start to play, I forget that I'm nervous, and it's really fun.

2 **Match.**

1	Did you have	a	go with?
2	What	b	performing?
3	Where	c	wear / take with you?
4	Who did you	d	did you go?
5	Did you like	e	a good weekend?
6	What did you	f	did you do?

3 **What are the two best weekend activities you have ever done?**

_____

_____

_____

_____

What can you remember about ... Unit 4?

1 **What are they doing? Complete.**

They are _____ a play.

2 **What is this craft activity called?**

_____

3 **What kind of game is this? Mark ✓.**

a board game ☐

a video game ☐

an outdoor game ☐

4 **What can you not do on a blog? Cross it out.**

express yourself   collect   comment

5 **Complete.**

I couldn't focus on what I was doing. I was d_____.

6 **What are they doing? Circle.**

paying attention   whispering   shaking hands

7 **Complete the question with *ever* or *never* and the present perfect. Then, answer.**

_____

she _____ (win) a competition?

_____

8 **Complete. Use the same word twice.**

Has Charlie slept out under the stars _____? No, not _____.

Read and complete with *also*, *too*, or *either*.

9 **Charlie learned to identify plants. He learned a lot about animals, _____.**

10 **He _____ learned how to make a campfire safely.**

Check your answers in the Student's Book. How did you do?

10 ☐ Wow!   8–9 ☐ Great!   6–7 ☐ Good!   0–5 ☐ Try harder!

? 😃 **How do we entertain ourselves?** Write your answer to the Big Question.

_____

_____

_____

5 What can history teach us?

1 ▶ 5.1 **Watch the video. Complete the graphic organizer.**

(clothes) (food) (work) (thinking) (fun)

what people _____

What can we learn from studying the past?

what people did _____

what people _____

what people _____

what _____ people did

2 Key Words 1 **Complete.**

> historical site   document   preserved   thousand   mosaic   century

This is a historical 1 _____.
It is from the 13th 2 _____.
It is not a 3 _____ of years old yet.

This is a 4 _____.
It is from Pompeii—a famous
5 _____. It is very well
6 _____.

Ready to Read: Nonfiction

1 Key Words 2 **Look and write.**

> bean   cinnamon   cacao tree   vanilla   chili   pod

a

b

c

d

e

f

2 **Complete with words from the box in Activity I.**

What Chocolate Comes From	Flavors

3 **Circle.**

a I don't like coffee—it tastes too **chili / bitter**.

b The most important ingredient in chocolate is the cacao **bean / tree**.

c To make a lot of chocolate, farmers had to plant a lot of cacao **pods / trees**.

d Adding **chili / beans** to chocolate makes it hot and spicy!

e Cacao and vanilla both have beans that grow in **pods / chili**.

f Sometimes, people add **cinnamon / pods** to chocolate to change the flavor.

1 **Read the title and look at the pictures to predict the main theme of the text. What is the main theme of the text? Circle.**

a spice markets around the world

b spices through history

c uses of spices today

Reading Strategy:
Identifying a Sequence of Events

The sequence is the order of events in an article or story. Knowing when things happen helps us understand a text.

2 **Read. Was your prediction correct? Circle.**

Yes / No

A SPICY JOURNEY

Spices are the seeds, fruit, roots, and skins of plants. They add flavor to all kinds of food—from vanilla ice cream to chili con carne. But can you imagine bathing in cinnamon? Or paying with pepper? What else have people used spices for through history? And where did spices come from?

The oldest written evidence of spices comes from ancient Egyptian, Chinese, and Indian civilizations. Ancient Egyptian documents from over 3,500 years ago list hundreds of herbs and spices—mainly used as medicines and to preserve meat.

Between 2,000 and 3,000 years ago, explorers from the Middle East went on expeditions to southern Asia. They brought back many spices, including cinnamon and black pepper. Traders from the Middle East then took spices to Europe, across the Mediterranean Sea.

In Europe, the Greeks and Romans used spices for medicine and cooking. They bathed in cinnamon, too. They also used spices as currency. Spices were very expensive—more valuable than gold at one time.

In the late 15th century, explorers from Spain and Portugal set off to discover cheaper spices. In 1493, Columbus brought chili to Europe from the Americas. Portuguese explorers then took chili with them to Asia. Like chili, vanilla traveled from the Americas to Asia, too.

Today, people all over the world cook with chili. It is one of the most popular spices, perhaps because it is hot but doesn't taste bitter. You can even buy chili-flavored chocolate—yum!

Chili Fact File

- Archeologists think that people in the Americas have eaten chili spice for more than 9,000 years.
- Almost half of the world's chili now comes from China.
- In Africa, farmers use chili to keep elephants away from their plants.
- Ice cream is better than water for cooling your mouth after eating hot chilli spice! Yay!

3 Read and number the events in the order they happened.

_____ a The Greeks and Romans used spices for medicine and washing.

_____ b People in the Americas started eating chili spice.

_____ c Ancient Egyptians wrote lists of herbs and spices.

_____ d Portuguese explorers took chili to Asia.

_____ e African farmers used chili to protect their plants.

_____ f Explorers from the Middle East brought back spices from southern Asia.

4 Read and write *T* (true), *F* (false), or *DK* (don't know).

a Elephants like vanilla. _____

b In Europe, people used to bathe in cinnamon. _____

c Spices were used to preserve meat. _____

d Pepper came from the Americas. _____

e Water is the best way to cool your mouth after eating chili. _____

f Spices were used like money. _____

g You can buy vanilla-flavored chocolate. _____

5 Read and complete.

a _____ are the seeds, fruit, skins, and roots of plants.

b Chili and _____ are spices from the Americas.

c Black pepper and _____ are spices from Asia.

d Almost half the world's chili now comes from _____.

e _____ is a spice that is often used to flavor ice cream.

f _____ might be one of the most popular spices because it doesn't taste bitter.

6 Read and answer.

a Do you like chili in your food? _____

b What other names of spices do you know in English?

_____

_____

c What is your favorite spice? _____

Present Perfect Questions with *How long*

We use *How long* and the present perfect to ask questions about something that started in the past and is still happening.

We use *for* and *since* to answer *How long … ?* questions. After *for*, we use a period of time. After *since*, we use a date or a particular point in time.

How long have **people** eaten **chili?** For **more than 9,000 years!**

How long has **chili** been **in Europe?** Since **the late 15th century.**

How long have **you** lived **on this street?** For **my whole life!**

How long has **your brother** collected **comics?** Since **he was six.**

1) **Complete the questions and circle the answers.**

a How long have you _____ (have) your bike?
   For / Since my birthday.

b How long has the World Wide Web _____ (exist)?
   For / Since around 30 years.

c How long have we _____ (be) at school today?
   For / Since 8:30 this morning.

d How long has your mom _____ (work) at the museum?
   For / Since three weeks.

e How long have people _____ (use) cinnamon in cooking?
   For / Since thousands of years!

f How long has she _____ (know) Peter?
   For / Since they were five years old.

2) **Write the time expressions in the table.**

> January   250 years   the 15th century   ten minutes   yesterday
> a week   11 o'clock   three days   2008   six months

For	Since

3) Complete with *For* or *Since*.

a How long have your parents been married? _____ 15 years.

b How long has Grandpa lived in Spain? _____ 1970.

c How long have we had our new car? _____ two weeks.

d How long has that building existed? _____ thousands of years.

e How long have I known my best friend? _____ our first day at school.

4) Read. Write questions with *How long* and the present perfect.

a How long / James Cameron / live / in the U.S.A.

_____

_____

b How long / he / work / in the movie industry

_____

_____

c How long / he / be / a movie director

_____

_____

d How long / he / be / a deep-sea explorer

_____

_____

e How long / Jessica Watson / sail

_____

_____

You've probably heard of some famous explorers from the 15th and 16th centuries, like Ferdinand Magellan and Vasco da Gama. But have you heard of these present-day explorers?

James Cameron – movie director (*Titanic*) and deep-sea diver

1954 – born August 16, in Ontario, Canada

1971 – moved to the U.S.A. with his family

1977 – started working in the movie industry as a writer

1978 – directed his first movie

1987 – became a deep-sea explorer while researching a film

Jessica Watson – sailor

1993 – born May 18, in Queensland, Australia

1998 – started sailing

2009–10 – sailed around the southern hemisphere alone at age 16

5) Answer the questions in Activity 4. Use both *For* and *Since*.

My Life

Answer for you. Use *For* or *Since*.

a How long have you been awake today? _____

b How long have you had your favorite toy or game? _____

c How long has your family lived in this village/town/city? _____

1 **Say and write the words. Underline _y_, _ie_, or _igh_.**

 a

 b

 c

_____

_____

_____

 d

 e

 f

_____

_____

_____

2 **Circle the word with the different vowel sound.**

a fly   fries   field

b science   ugly   sky

c pie   high   piece

d try   tasty   bright

e windy   why   die

f magpie   eight   firefighter

Oracy

1 **Read. Underline three phrases that encourage someone to participate in the discussion.**

Jack My friend Chris is coming to visit this weekend. Where should we take him?

Kate That's awesome. Well, we should go to the market square to show him the cool toy stand there … What do you think, Liam?

Liam Well, he needs to see the old palace, because it's really interesting and not every town has its own palace!

Jack Great idea, Liam. Do you agree, Emma?

Emma I'm not sure. The old palace is nice, but maybe we could visit the castle, too. It's fun to go there in the evening when it's dark!

Liam Yes, that's true! What about you, Jack? What do you think?

Jack My favorite place is the Roman ruins near the market. So maybe we could go to the market first, then see the ruins, and then go to the palace and finally the castle!

All Great!

Why / Why don't ? Because …

We ask questions with *why* when we want to know the reason for something.
We usually answer *why* questions with *because* followed by the reason.

Why did only rich Mayans drink chocolate?
Because cacao beans were very expensive.

Why is this chocolate sweet?
Because it has honey in it.

Why aren't you working on your project?
Because I'm doing my math homework first.

We can also use *why don't* to make suggestions. If we can't or don't want to do
what someone suggests, we can use *because* to give a reason.

Why don't you come to the museum with us?
I'd love to, but I can't because **I'm visiting my cousins.**

1 Match.

1 Why should you visit the theater?   a Because I've seen it three times already!

2 Why do you like studying history?   b Because I finished it!

3 Why don't you drink coffee?   c Because I have a soccer tournament.

4 Why don't you want to see the movie?   d Because you'll love it!

5 Why don't you have your book?   e Because I like learning about the past.

6 Why don't you come to the party?   f Because I don't like it—it's too bitter.

2 Look. Answer the questions with Because …

 Why are the
children cold?

_____

_____

 Why is the girl
happy?

Because _____

_____

 Why is the boy
upset?

_____

_____

 Why are they
scared?

_____

_____

1 READ Answer the question.

What can you make in the museum? _____

2 PLAN Prepare to write a brochure for a museum. Think of a museum you know and like. Complete the graphic organizer.

Why visit? What can you do?

- _____
- _____
- _____

Where?	Price
_____	_____

One suggestion

Why don't you _____ ?

3 WRITE Use the graphic organizer to write and design your brochure in your notebooks.

4 EDIT Did you ...

☐ include the address?

☐ include the price?

☐ include what you can do there?

☐ use *Why?* / *Why don't?* and *because* correctly?

Travel Back in Time
at Our Amazing Museum!

There's so much to explore at the National History Museum. Why visit us?

Because ...

🐾 you can follow the footprints and spot the dinosaurs hiding in our prehistoric park. Learn about the archeology of our region with our robot guides.

🐾 you can discover the history of planes and trains and make your own airplanes in our transportation room.

🐾 you can learn about the history of computers in our technology room. Why not try writing a simple computer program?

🐾 in our 3D movie theater, you can watch movies about the history of the region. It's like stepping into the past!

Why should you come? Because you will love it!

Where to find us: 21 Broad Street, Portland
Price: Children $8   Adults $12

1 Key Words 4 **Complete.**

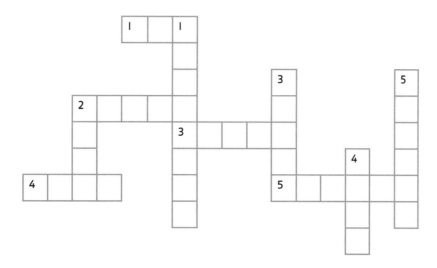

Across

1 Something you do with your fingers or an eraser

2 To look at something for a long time

3 Not neat

4 Things that don't work and are not worth a lot

5 To show something that was hidden before

Down

1 The underground floor of a house

2 To use a machine to put a picture of a document into a computer

3 One thickness or level of something, e.g., of snow or cake

4 A pile

5 A bit cold

2 **Complete.**

> messy   heap   layer   scan   reveal   rub

a Please could you _____ this document for me? I need to send it by email.

b Mom says my room is too _____. I have to clean up before I can go to the party.

c If you _____ two sticks together, you can start a fire.

d My sister never puts her clothes away—she leaves them in a _____ on the floor.

e Archeologists _____ the secrets of the past.

f She found the artifact under a _____ of mud.

1 **Look. What do you think happened to the building?**

_____

2 **Read. Were your answers to Activity I right?**

Reading Strategy: Identifying Cause and Effect

When we read, we think about why something happened. We can see what events (causes) prompt other things to happen (effects).

Layers of History

Pablo stared at the wall of the house in front of him. They were on a family vacation to New York. He was excited about seeing the Empire State Building and visiting the Intrepid Sea, Air, and Space Museum. But he was not so excited about visiting the apartment where his dad's grandma lived when she first came to the city.

Now that they were here, he was even less excited. All that was left of the building was one wall and a pile of bricks.

"Dad, did you know before we came that it was going to be just a heap of junk?" Pablo asked.

"No. I didn't know they were going to knock down her building to build a new one. In fact, I haven't been back since my grandma died, 20 years ago." They looked in silence for a while. Then, Pablo spoke.

"The top layer of paint is green, but there's some white underneath. And I can see a bit of orange, too. It's funny—each layer is like a different part of somebody's life."

"Like layers of rock under the ground," said his sister Ana.

"Well, I suppose we're a bit like archeologists," said Dad, "except we're looking at the history of one building, instead of an ancient civilization."

"When did your grandma move here?" asked Ana.

"She came here in 1925, when she was just five years old. A lot of other families arrived around the same time, from Ireland, Italy, Eastern Europe, parts of Latin America … they all wanted to make new lives in New York."

"Did she know any of the other families?"

"Oh, yes—she met my grandpa here!"

"So it's kind of a historical site for our family!" said Pablo. "Can we take a brick home?"

3 **Read again and circle the best summary—*a*, *b*, or *c*.**

a Pablo and his family visit his dad's grandma while they are on a family vacation in New York. Pablo learns some things about his family.

b Pablo and his family visit the apartment where his dad's grandma lived while they are on a family vacation in New York. They go inside and learn some things about their family.

c Pablo and his family visit the apartment where his dad's grandma lived while they are on a family vacation in New York. It isn't there, but Pablo learns some things about his family.

4 **Match the cause to the effect.**

Cause

1 People wanted to make new lives in New York.

2 The family was going to see the Empire State Building and visit the Sea, Air, and Space Museum.

3 All that was left of the building was a wall and some bricks.

4 The family was going to the place where Pablo's dad's grandma had lived.

5 Pablo saw different layers of paint on the remaining wall.

Effect

a Pablo was excited.

b A lot of families arrived around the same time, from Europe and Latin America.

c Pablo was not so excited.

d Dad, Pablo, and Ana felt a bit like archeologists.

e Pablo thought it looked like a heap of junk.

5 **What happened when? Complete with a time phrase.**

> in 1925   for a long time   20 years ago
> around the same time   since his grandma died

a Pablo's dad's grandma came to New York _____.

b A lot of other families arrived _____.

c She died _____.

d Pablo's dad hasn't been back to the apartment _____.

e He hasn't been there _____.

Present Perfect (for/since) vs. Past Simple

I haven't been **here for a long time.**
He hasn't been **back since his grandma died.**
We've lived **in this house since I was born.**

I went **to the museum yesterday.**
She came **here in 1925.**
They visited **the historical site last week.**

1 **Complete with *for* or *since*.**

a Dinosaurs have been extinct _____ millions of years.
b I haven't watched TV _____ the weekend.
c We haven't been on vacation _____ a long time.
d I'm really hungry—I haven't eaten _____ this morning!
e People have drunk hot chocolate _____ thousands of years.
f The museum hasn't been open _____ last month.

2 **Which phrases can you use with the present perfect and the past simple? Complete.**

> for three years   since June   never   when I was five   since last week
> 100 years ago   in 2002   for a long time   last night   yesterday   this week
> today   for two months   since 1948   in the 20th century   since I was a child

Present Perfect

_____
_____
_____
_____

_____
_____
_____
_____
_____

Past Simple

_____
_____
_____
_____
_____

3 Complete with the present perfect or past simple.

a We _____ (have) chocolate bars for around 170 years.

b Chocolate makers _____ (make) the first chocolate bar in the 1850s.

c We _____ (enjoy) eating chocolate bars ever since!

d A volcano _____ (destroy) the Roman city of Pompeii 2,000 years ago.

e An Italian architect _____ (discover) the ruins of Pompeii in the 16th century.

f Archeologists _____ (explore) the historical site of Pompeii since 1748.

4 Read and complete with the present perfect or past simple.

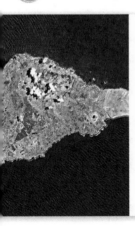

Easter Island is 2,300 miles off the west coast of Chile, in the Pacific Ocean. Dutch explorers 1 _____ (land) there in 1722, but there were already people living there. The first people to live there 2 _____ (call) it "Rapa Nui." They 3 _____ (build) some very large stone statues called "moai." But no one is sure why! Easter Island 4 _____ (be) a UNESCO World Heritage Site since 1995.

5 Read and write sentences with the present perfect and past simple.

a Write about an activity you have done for a long time.

I have _____ **for / since** _____.

I started _____.

b Write about something you haven't done for a long time.

I haven't _____ **for / since** _____.

The last time I _____.

1 **Look and complete.**

	Do you think we can learn about this from older people?	Have you ever spoken with an older person about this?
The place your family comes from		
The food people used to eat		
The food people eat in different countries		
The toys people used to play with		
Different ways of thinking about life		

2 **Which are questions we can ask an older person to find out about the past? Look and mark ✓.**

a Where were you born? ☐

b Can you show me some photos of the town you grew up in? ☐

c Can we watch TV now? ☐

d What did you use to eat? ☐

e Can you show me how to cook that recipe from your childhood? ☐

f Are you really old? ☐

g I have a problem. What do you think I should do? ☐

h What toys did you use to play with? ☐

3 **Write two more questions you would like to ask an older person to find out about the past.**

_____

_____

4 **Why is learning about the past from our an older person important?**

_____

_____

_____

Check Your Oracy!

1 I used the phrases on the cue cards.
   All of them / Some of them / None of them

2 I participated in the discussion.
   All the time / Sometimes / Never

3 If other members of my group didn't participate,
   I encouraged them to do so. **Yes / No**

How can we talk about how life has changed?

The Big Challenge

1 **Color the stars to give yourself a score.***

I thought of lots of ideas.	☆☆☆☆☆
I gave reasons for my ideas.	☆☆☆☆☆
I participated in the choice of three ideas.	☆☆☆☆☆
I practiced presenting my group's idea(s).	☆☆☆☆☆
I presented my group's idea(s) to the class.	☆☆☆☆☆
I listened to the other groups' presentations.	☆☆☆☆☆

*(5 = Awesome! 4 = Pretty good, 3 = OK, 2 = Could be better, 1 = Needs more work!)

2 **Which idea did you like best? Why?**

_____

_____

The Big Question and **Me**

Because of the things I have learned in this unit,

1 I will _____.

2 I will _____.

1 **Circle.**

a The year 1742 was in the 18th **thousand / century**.

b Vasco da Gama was a famous **explorer / civilization**. He was Portuguese.

c The historian held the **documents / mosaics** carefully—the paper was very thin.

d Some artifacts from Pompeii were perfectly **explored / preserved**.

e The ruins of Teotihuacan, in Mexico, are over a **thousand / century** years old.

f Ancient Greece and Ancient Rome were ancient European **civilizations / mosaics**.

2 **Complete.**

> beans   chili   bitter   popular   cacao tree   flavor

a We use spices to add _____ to food.

b Cacao grows on the _____ .

c To make chocolate, you need sugar, milk, cocoa butter, and cacao

_____ .

d If you add _____ to chocolate, it tastes spicy.

e Without sugar, chocolate tastes _____ .

f Chocolate became very _____ in Europe in the 17th century.

3 **Circle.**

1 It's not very warm today—I feel quite _____ .

  a chilly **b** messy **c** chili

2 Do you need this, or is it _____ ?

  a heap **b** layer **c** junk

3 Could you go down to the _____ and sort through your old toys?

  a layer **b** basement **c** heap

4 Turn off your tablet! You need to stop _____ at a screen!

  a scanning **b** rubbing **c** staring

5 Under the dust, the archeologist _____ some old coins.

  a stared **b** revealed **c** scanned

6 Can you _____ this document on your printer?

  a scan **b** rub **c** reveal

(4) Make questions with the present perfect. Complete the answers with *For* or *Since*.

a How long _____ (you / have) your bike?

   _____ last month.

b How long _____ (she / work) as a historian?

   _____ two years.

c How long _____ (this mosaic / exist)?

   _____ hundreds of years.

d How long _____ (they / play) together as a team?

   _____ September.

e How long _____ (people / use) cell phones?

   _____ 1973.

f How long _____ (you / know) the news?

   _____ a few hours.

(5) Complete with the present perfect or past simple.

Not all historical sites are thousands of years old or full of
grand buildings or statues. The Tenement Museum in New York
1 _____ (be) the idea of a historian, Ruth Abram.
She wanted to preserve the history of people who
2 _____ (come) to the city to start new lives in
the 19th and 20th centuries. The museum 3 _____
(open) in 1992 with one restored apartment. Since then, it
4 _____ (tell) the stories of the people who lived
there to thousands of visitors every year. It 5 _____
(become) a very popular museum, and it 6 _____ (grow), too.
It now has seven restored apartments in one building.

(6) Match.

1 Why did Ruth Abram want to open a museum?

2 Why did people come to New York?

3 Why don't you want to come to the museum?

4 Why do you want to go to the history museum?

a Because I have a soccer tournament.

b Because I like finding out how people lived in the past.

c Because they wanted to start new lives.

d Because she wanted to tell the stories of people who came to New York.

SPEAKING MISSION

1 **What did they say?**
Complete the conversation.

schedule   low season   attractions   group tour
tour guides   high season   private tour

Jeremy Terrific Tours Australia. How can I help you?

Sofia Hi. We are looking for family tours with kids. Can you please give me information on some tours around Sydney?

Jeremy Of course. What I _____ are you interested in?

Sofia Mmm ... we are interested in Luna Park, Taronga Zoo, and the SEA LIFE Sydney Aquarium.

Jeremy One moment, please ... We have a day tour to Luna Park and Taronga Zoo.

Sofia That sounds great.

Jeremy Do you want a walking tour with a ferry ride or a bus tour?

Sofia A walking tour with a ferry ride.

Jeremy Do you prefer a 2 _____ or a 3 _____?

Sofia A group tour.

Jeremy Great.

Sofia How much does it cost?

Jeremy In 4 _____, it's usually $629 for a family of four. But, you are in luck. It is currently 5 _____, which means it comes down to $359.

Sofia Wow. That's great. How long does the tour last?

Jeremy Six hours. I'll give you the 6 _____.

Sofia What time does the tour start?

Jeremy It starts at 9:45 a.m.

Sofia Great. Thank you.

Jeremy What language would you like the tour in? We have 7 _____ who speak English, Spanish, Chinese ...

2 **Match.**

1 Hello. Can you please
2 What attractions
3 Do you want / prefer
4 How much
5 How long
6 What language

a does it cost?
b does the tour last?
c give me information on tours of ...?
d would you like the tour in?
e are you interested in?
f a walking tour or a bus tour? / a private tour or a group tour?

What can you remember about ... Unit 5?

1 **What is this?**

_____

2 **What is Pompeii? Circle.**

a document   a historical site
an explorer

3 **What is this? Complete.**

Cacao beans in a

_____ .

4 **Which one is not a spice?
Cross it out.**

cinnamon   currency   vanilla

5 **What part of the
house is this?**

_____

6 **Which pictures
show layers? Mark ✓ two.**

7 **Circle.**

How long have people drunk hot
chocolate in North America?
For / Since 4,000 years.

8 **Complete with the present
perfect or past simple.**

Children _____
(play) with marbles for thousands
of years. In the 1850s, people
_____ (start) making
marbles from glass.

Read and answer with *because*.

9 **Why is he on
the island?**

_____
_____

10 **Why does the sailor give him
some soap?** _____

Check your answers in the Student's Book. How did you do?
10 ☐ Wow!   8–9 ☐ Great!   6–7 ☐ Good!   0–5 ☐ Try harder!

? 😃 **What can history teach us?** Write your answer to the Big Question.

_____
_____
_____

6 Where does food come from?

1 ▶ 6.1 **Watch the video. Complete the graphic organizer.**

> chicken pineapples eggs apples milk peaches yogurt corn
> tomatoes cheese sugar butter bananas turkey tea coffee

Where does our food come from?

Food from Plants	Food from Animals

2 Key Words 1 **Complete.**

> sugarcane livestock orchards processed food
> greenhouses plantations saturated fats dairy products

a Some farms have _____—fields full of fruit trees.

b _____ protect sensitive plants from rain, wind, and cold.

c Tea, coffee, bananas, and _____ often grow on bigger farms.

d We call bigger farms in hot countries _____.

e Cheese, butter, and yogurt are all _____.

f _____ is another name for farm animals.

g Food made in factories is _____.

h _____ are not very good for us.

1 [Key Words 2] **Match.**

1	import	a	information about the ingredients in your food
2	package	b	recently picked or prepared, still good to eat
3	food label	c	to become bad to eat
4	throw away	d	food that people still haven't eaten at the end of a meal
5	spoil	e	to bring something into a country from another country to sell
6	fresh	f	a container for the food or other things you buy
7	leftovers	g	to put something in the garbage because you don't want it

2 **Circle.**

1 The _____ can tell you how much sugar is in your food.

   a leftovers **b** package **c** food label

2 The U.K. _____ most of its food from other countries.

   a spoils **b** imports **c** throws away

3 You can open that _____ of cookies later.

   a food label **b** leftovers **c** package

4 If food gets too old, it _____.

   a spoils **b** imports **c** throws away

5 _____ can be really tasty the next day.

   a Packages **b** Leftovers **c** Food labels

6 We had to _____ some rice because we cooked too much.

   a throw away **b** spoil **c** import

1 **Look. What do you think the article is about?** _____

2 **Read. Circle the theme of the article.**

a food labels

b leftovers

c processed food

> **Reading Strategy:** Identifying Author's Purpose
>
> When you read a text, it's important to identify the writer's message.

HOME   BLOG   RECIPES   CONTACT

Pizza for Breakfast?!

Have you ever eaten cold pizza for breakfast? Some people think pizza tastes better the day after you make it. Why do some leftovers—but not others—taste better the next day?

Well, some foods keep better than others. Cold can damage many fruits and vegetables, like bananas, lemons, and tomatoes. And fresh foods, like vegetables and lettuce, don't stay fresh after you cut them. Being out in the air makes them spoil. Rice and seafood don't keep very well, either. Bacteria inside them can start to grow, so eating these foods when they are old can make you sick.

But some cooked foods, like stews, curries, and chili con carne, can taste better the next day—and even better two days later. These foods usually contain onion, garlic, and herbs or spices. When you cook, these ingredients react with protein in the food. They give the food its flavor. They can continue to add flavor while the food is cooling, and even in the refrigerator.

Scientists think pizza tastes better the next day because the tomatoes stop water from getting into the crust. Also, fat and water do not mix. The fat in the cheese helps it to stay separate on top—and the whole thing still tastes yummy!

So, the next time you make too much food, what will you do? Think before you throw it away. You could have tasty leftovers for breakfast, lunch, or dinner. Just remember these simple rules to stay safe:

- Cool leftovers for no more than two hours if possible. Then, put them in the refrigerator.
- Only reheat leftovers once.
- Use your leftovers in two or three days.

You can also make your leftovers into something else! <u>Why not try these simple recipes</u>?

SB pages 118–121

3 What does the the writer want to do?
Mark ✓ three purposes of the text.

a to show you how to make pizza ☐

b to advise you about how to store
leftovers safely ☐

c to tell you about the history of spices ☐

d to explain why some food tastes better
the day after you cook it ☐

e to encourage you not to waste food ☐

f to give you ideas for growing
your own food ☐

g to give you recipes for leftovers ☐

4 Read and circle *T* (true) or *F* (false).

a Not all food tastes better the next day.   **T   F**

b You should always store fruit in the refrigerator.   **T   F**

c Food containing herbs and spices often tastes better the day after cooking. **T   F**

d Cheese contains fat.   **T   F**

e You should let food cool overnight before you store it in the refrigerator.   **T   F**

f If you store them in the refrigerator, leftovers are safe to eat for two weeks. **T   F**

g Being out in the air makes some foods go bad.   **T   F**

5 Read and answer.

a Have you ever eaten pizza for breakfast? _____

b Do you ever eat leftovers the next day? _____

c Do you know any meals that use up leftovers? Write them here.

Indefinite Pronouns

You could make your leftovers into **something** else.

Is there **anything** in the fridge? I'm really hungry!

Oh, no—there's **nothing** in the pan! Did you eat **everything**?

Wow—**someone** made an amazing cake!

Is **anyone** hungry? Dad cooked lots of spaghetti!

I called the restaurant, but **no one** answered.

The party is over—**everyone**'s gone home.

1 Circle.

a Can I please have **anything / something** to eat?

b The cupboard is empty—there's **nothing / anything** there!

c Shhhh! Don't say **nothing / anything**!

d There are no leftovers—we ate **anything / everything**.

e Do you know **anyone / no one** who likes baking?

f I think there's **someone / anyone** at the door.

g I looked, but there's **everyone / no one** there.

h I really want to go to the party—**anyone / everyone** in my class is going.

2 Match.

1 Thea's party was amazing—_____ wanted to leave!

2 We're going to cook _____ special for Mom's birthday.

3 I met _____ who doesn't like ice cream!

4 Do you know _____ about the movie?

5 _____ likes chili except me!

6 Has _____ seen the ketchup?

7 Do we have _____ we need to bake the cake?

8 We finished the meal—there's _____ left.

a everyone

b someone

c anyone

d no one

e nothing

f anything

g something

h everything

SB page 122

3) Complete with an indefinite pronoun.

> something   someone   everything   everyone
> no one   anything   nothing   anyone

a We have _____ to do tonight—there's no homework.

b _____ gave me a great recipe for using up leftovers.

c There must be _____ we can do to waste less food.

d I don't know _____ who is going to the party.

e The house next door is empty at the moment—_____ lives there.

f The cooking class is free—it doesn't cost _____ .

g I ate _____ in my lunchbox. It was delicious!

h _____ can try to throw away less food.

4) Make sentences and questions.

a enjoyed / the / meal / Everyone

_____

b didn't / me / Sam / anything / to / say

_____

c this / anyone's / Is / seat

_____

d for ten minutes / I / but / waited / came / no one

_____

e everything / for the party / ready / Is

_____

f Someone / ate / cake / my

_____

My Life

Complete for you.

a Everyone in my family likes _____ .

b No one I know has a _____ .

c Someone who I think is amazing is _____ .

Spelling Patterns and Word Study

1 Say and write the words. Underline *oo*, *ou*, or *o*.

You _____ drink something!

What _____ you like?

2 Circle the word with the different vowel sound.

a book   foot   food   d would   wood   pool

b wolf   took   wool   e old   wolf   woman

c cold   could   woman   f should   school   could

Oracy

1 Write details about your plan for your school garden and what you will grow there.

_____

_____

_____

2 What reasons did you give for growing those things or for how you planned your garden?

_____

_____

3 What phrases did you use to support your argument?

_____

_____

Adjective Order

When more than one adjective comes before a noun, the adjectives are normally in a particular order.

1	2	3	4	5
opinion	size	physical description	age	color
beautiful	little	shiny	new	gold

But you don't normally use five adjectives!

beautiful shiny new blue shoes

1 Mark ✓ the correct order of adjectives.

1 **a** I love tasty big green apples. ☐

  b I love tasty green big apples. ☐

2 **a** Look at Ella's new black awesome boots! ☐

  b Look at Ella's awesome new black boots! ☐

3 **a** There's a pretty little blue bird in the garden. ☐

  b There's a pretty blue little bird in the garden. ☐

4 **a** Mmm … have you tried those orange amazing little pumpkin pies? ☐

  b Mmm … have you tried those amazing little orange pumpkin pies? ☐

2 Look. Write descriptions.

white new cool

Have you seen my

_____

sneakers?

red big juicy

Mmm … I love

_____

strawberries!

blue old faded

Dad really
loves his

_____

denim jacket.

red and pink enormous amazing

Wow! Look at that

_____

cake!

1 READ   Answer the question.

How often do they bake the bread that they sell? _____

1

Gemma's Juice

Bringing you the best fruits from local farms

These healthy juices will wake you up in the morning!

Our delicious new Green Kiwi juice is on sale—20% off!

2

Fred's Bread

It's freshly baked and tastes great!

We have bread in all shapes and sizes. It's baked in the store every day. Come and try our tasty new peanut loaf now!

2 PLAN   Prepare to write an ad for a food product. Complete the graphic organizer.

What is it?
_____

What's good about it?
(Think of at least three things)

- _____
- _____
- _____

Think of a Slogan
_____
_____
_____

Design a Logo

3 WRITE   Use the graphic organizer to write and design your ad in your notebooks.

4 EDIT   Did you ...

☐ include a logo?
☐ include a slogan?
☐ include things that are good about your product?
☐ order adjectives correctly?

Unit 6B — Ready to Read: Fiction

1 Key Words 4 **Complete.**

> bite   harmless   pests   quarantine   produce (n)   produce (v)

a Animals sometimes have to stay in _____ when they move to a new country.

b We buy fresh local _____ from the market.

c The farmer's orchards _____ very tasty apples.

d The spider looked scary, but it was _____ .

e It's OK, my dog doesn't _____ .

f Insects and spiders are common fruit _____ .

2 **Find the words!**

> flyswatter
> produce
> bite
> inject
> pest
> quarantine
> fang
> harmless
> cockroach

R	S	S	E	L	M	R	A	H	R
C	E	Q	N	C	P	E	S	T	E
O	T	T	I	U	U	P	A	T	E
C	C	X	T	F	M	D	I	A	M
K	E	E	N	A	A	B	O	E	O
R	J	I	A	L	W	N	C	R	W
O	N	H	R	B	Y	S	G	O	P
A	I	W	A	P	V	U	Y	X	P
C	V	T	U	E	T	Y	H	L	J
H	A	T	Q	Y	D	N	A	E	F

1. **Look. What do you think they are going to do?** _____

2. **Read. Was your answer to Activity I right?** _____

> **Reading Strategy:** Open vs. Closed Questions
>
> Open questions are questions that can't be answered with *yes* or *no*.
> Open questions usually start with *why*, *how*, *who*, *when*, *where*, or *what*.
> Asking these questions can help you understand a text in more detail.

A Rainy-Day Picnic

Lucy looked out of the window. The rain wasn't going to stop any time soon.

"We aren't picking strawberries today, are we?" she said to her brother, Max.

"Hmm … I don't think so," said Max disappointedly.

Their dad was planning to take Lucy and Max to a fruit farm. They were going to pick some local produce and have a picnic. But now they would have to wait until another day for their special trip.

Suddenly, Max jumped up from the floor where he was playing.

"Why don't we have an indoor picnic?" he said.

"That's a great idea," said Dad. "If you go and get a blanket, I'll start making sandwiches."

"But we won't be able to make a fruit salad," said Lucy.

"Yes, we will— we have some apples in the fruit bowl.

And there's some orange juice in the fridge. Here, take this knife and chop the apples into small pieces."

Lucy started chopping, happy that they had a plan. Then, suddenly, she stopped.

"Dad! Look!" She pointed at a large hole inside the apple. "Something has already eaten it."

"Ah … it's probably a sawfly or a type of moth. They're really common apple pests— they're annoying but harmless."

"Why don't the farmers use something to kill the pests?"

"Well, they could, but it might kill the animals that eat the pests, too. And if those animals disappear, there's nothing to control the pests naturally. A pest isn't a bad animal—it's just an animal that's somewhere we don't want it to be!"

"Like Floppy!" said Max, returning with a thick blanket and pointing out of the window. Floppy was Lucy and Max's pet rabbit. She was sitting right in the middle of their vegetable garden, biting into one of the carrots that was growing there!

SB pages 127–132

3 **Are the questions open or closed? Write O or C. Then, write the answers.**

a Was it raining? _____

_____

b Where was Lucy and Max's dad planning to take them? _____

_____

c Who suggested having an indoor picnic instead? _____

_____

d Did they pick strawberries? _____

_____

e What did Lucy start making? _____

_____

4 **Complete the questions. Then, write the answers.**

How   Who   Where   Why   What

a _____ was Lucy happy?

_____

b _____ did Lucy find in the apple?

_____

c _____ did it get there?

_____

d _____ gets the picnic blanket?

_____

e _____ is Floppy sitting?

_____

5 **What do think? Write your answers.**

a Have you ever grown your own produce? _____

b What are some common pests in your country? _____

c In the story, do you think Floppy is a pest? _____

Grammar in Context

Tag Questions

In spoken English, we often add short questions at the end of a sentence to check information, emphasize a point, or ask if someone agrees with us.

I'm good at baking, aren't I?
She's a waiter, isn't she?
We aren't going shopping, are we?
You don't like coffee, do you?
Britain imports a lot of tea, doesn't it?
They eat meat, don't they?
You ate the leftovers, didn't you?
It wasn't sunny, was it?
We didn't pick strawberries today, did we?
There isn't any homework, is there?

1) **Circle.**

a Bananas spoil in the fridge, **don't they / doesn't it?**

b There are sugarcane plantations in the Caribbean, **aren't there / are there?**

c He's a livestock farmer, **doesn't he / isn't he?**

d We're going out for lunch, **don't we / aren't we?**

e You haven't been to the store yet, **have you / haven't you?**

f Processed food often contains saturated fats, **isn't it / doesn't it?**

2) **Match.**

1 Apples float in water,	a aren't they?
2 That's a cockroach,	b has it?
3 He doesn't work in the orchard,	c did they?
4 It hasn't rained,	d aren't I?
5 Our cousins are coming for dinner,	e don't they?
6 I'm not the youngest,	f am I?
7 They didn't plant carrots in their garden,	g does he?
8 I'm the tallest,	h isn't it?

114

(3) Complete with a tag question.

a She's Mexican, _____ ?

b There aren't any strawberries, _____ ?

c They live on our street, _____ ?

d Your brother doesn't eat dairy products, _____ ?

e You haven't tasted the cake yet, _____ ?

f We cooked enough food for everyone, _____ ?

(4) Complete the first part of each sentence.

_____ late, are we?

_____ first, aren't I?

_____ finished, haven't you?

_____ any milk, is there?

_____ (need) some water, doesn't she?

Dairy products _____ (grow) in greenhouses, do they?

(5) Read and complete the sentences to make them true for you.

a I'm _____ , aren't I?

b I'm not _____ , am I?

c I _____ , don't I?

d I don't _____ , do I?

1 **Look and complete.**

	Do you think this is a good decision?	
	Yes ✓	No ✗
Growing your own vegetables		
Buying local produce		
Using leftovers to make another meal		
Buying more food than you need		
Buying fair-trade produce		

2 **Who is making a good decision about the food they buy? Look and mark ✓.**

a I had to throw away half of the salad because I bought too much! ☐

b We don't have a big garden, but I'm growing some herbs on my kitchen windowsill. ☐

c I made an awesome curry from the leftovers at lunch. ☐

d We're going to the farmers' market to buy some ingredients for dinner. ☐

e I always check food labels to see where my food comes from. ☐

3 **Why is making better decisions about the food we buy important?**

_____

_____

_____

Check Your Oracy!

1 I participated in the discussion.   **Yes / No**

2 I supported my arguments with evidence.   **All the time / Sometimes / Never**

3 I used the phrases on the cue cards.   **All of them / Some of them / None of them**

> **How can we make better decisions about the foods we buy?**

The Big Challenge

1 Color the stars to give yourself a score.*

I researched—on the Internet and in other ways.	☆☆☆☆☆
I participated in choosing the meal to present.	☆☆☆☆☆
I helped to prepare my group's presentation.	☆☆☆☆☆
I practiced presenting my group's meal plan.	☆☆☆☆☆
I presented my group's meal plan to the class.	☆☆☆☆☆
I listened to the other groups' presentations.	☆☆☆☆☆

*(5 = Awesome! 4 = Pretty good, 3 = OK, 2 = Could be better, 1 = Needs more work!)

2 Which meal plan did you like best? Why?

_____

_____

The Big Question and   **Me**

Because of the things I have learned in this unit,

1 I will _____.

2 I will _____.

1 Circle.

a Farmers grow tea and coffee on large **orchards / plantations**.

b **Dairy products / Processed foods** include milk, butter, and cheese.

c Some farmers have **orchards / greenhouses** of fruit trees on their farms.

d **Saturated fats / Processed foods** often contain a lot of salt, sugar, and fat.

e **Greenhouses / Plantations** are useful for protecting produce like tomatoes.

f Cows, sheep, and pigs are **sugarcane / livestock**.

2 Complete.

> import   package   food label   throw away   spoil   fresh   leftovers

a If you want to know where your food comes from, look at the _____.

b I prefer _____ vegetables to processed vegetables—they taste better and are healthier.

c Many countries _____ coffee from Brazil.

d Do you know any recipes for using up _____?

e Does milk _____ quickly?

f Can I open this _____ of pasta?

g Don't _____ that pizza—we can have it for lunch tomorrow!

3 Circle.

1 Mom chased the insect around the kitchen with a _____!

   a fang   **b** bite   **c** flyswatter

2 They put the sick dog in _____ to keep the other animals safe.

   a cockroach   **b** quarantine   **c** pest

3 Some spiders can _____ poison into you!

   a inject   **b** produce   **c** bite

4 Some snakes and spiders have sharp _____.

   a pests   **b** fangs   **c** produce

5 A _____ is a brown or black insect sometimes found in houses.

   a flyswatter   **b** cockroach   **c** quarantine

6 The farmer's orchard _____ a lot of fruit.

   a produces   **b** bites   **c** injects

4 Complete with an indefinite pronoun.

This weekend, we're going to have a surprise party for my grandma's 70th birthday. She doesn't know 1 _____ about it. My cousins and I planned it. We are going to play games and have cake. 2 _____ is going to bring 3 _____ to eat, so there will be lots of food. I hope 4 _____ forgets! We still need to find 5 _____ to play the piano when we sing "Happy Birthday." Apart from that, I think we've remembered 6 _____—and I hope we haven't forgotten to invite 7 _____ !

5 Complete the tag questions.

a This food is fresh, _____?

b There aren't any apples in the fruit bowl, _____?

c Families waste a lot of food at home, _____?

d She doesn't like eggs, _____?

e We've been to that restaurant, _____?

f You haven't cooked this before, _____?

6 Look. Write descriptions.

a

black   cool   new
Do you like my
_____
jeans?

b

old   dirty   brown
Shall I throw away those
_____
boots?

c

green   beautiful bright   big
The banana tree has
_____
_____
leaves.

1 Read and answer.

a Who was on your team?

_____

b What was the name of your video game?

_____

c What does your video game teach?

_____

_____

d What features and effects make it interesting for fourth graders?

_____

_____

_____

2 What are the speakers doing? Write _a_, _b_, or _c_.

a expressing opinions   b eliciting contributions from others

c giving evidence to support an argument

1 I think eating leftovers the next day is a bad idea. _____

2 I disagree because it's safe, and some food tastes better the next day—like pizza! _____

3 What do you think, Emma? _____

3 What did you say? Write examples.

a expressing an opinion

_____

b eliciting contributions from others

_____

c giving evidence to support an argument

_____

What can you remember about ... Unit 6?

1 **What plant is this?**

_____

2 **Where is the plant in Activity I growing? Circle.**

an orchard   a plantation
a greenhouse

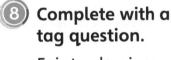

3 **What is this part of the package called?**

_____

4 **Which is the odd one out? Cross it out.**

import   spoil   go bad

5 **What is he using?**

_____
_____

6 **Complete.**

Don't worry, that spider won't hurt you—it's _____ .

7 **Circle.**

Would **someone / anyone / no one** like a cookie?

8 **Complete with a tag question.**

Fair trade gives farmers a fair price for their produce, _____ ?

9 **Mark ✓ the correct sentence.**

The waiter is wearing a white nice clean shirt. ☐

The waiter is wearing a nice clean white shirt. ☐

10 **Write the words in the correct order.**

black   short   neat

The waiter has

_____ hair.

Check your answers in the Student's Book. How did you do?

10 ☐ Wow!   8–9 ☐ Great!   6–7 ☐ Good!   0–5 ☐ Try harder!

? 😀 **Where does food come from?** Write your answer to the Big Question.

_____

_____

_____

7 Why is water important?

1 ▶ 7.1 **Watch the video. Complete the graphic organizer.**

washing   cooking   electricity   drinking   leisure activities   agriculture

for _____,
to keep us alive

to make
_____, for
energy

for _____,
to grow food

Water as a
resource—what do
we use it for?

for _____,
to have fun

for _____,
to be clean

for _____
our food

2 Key Words 1 **Complete.**

involve   fresh water   valuable   water shortage
wetland   conserve   irrigation

a Water is a _____ resource.

b Many human activities _____ some use of water.

c In dry countries, farmers use _____ systems to water their crops.

d Some animals live in _____ habitats—streams, rivers, and lakes.

e Other animals, like crocodiles and alligators, live in _____ areas.

f When it doesn't rain for a long time, we say there is a _____.

g We can all do something to _____ water.

Ready to Read: Nonfiction

1 Key Words 2 **Look and write.**

bridge   dam
swamp   canal
ditch   wave (n)
island

_____

_____

_____

_____

_____

_____

_____

2 **Match.**

1 a wall across a river or lake, to hold in water   a wave

2 a waterway made for irrigation or for boats to travel on   b island

3 something to carry a road, railway, or path over a river   c ditch

4 a long, narrow, open hole made at the side of a field or road   d swamp

5 a piece of land with water on every side   e dam

6 an area of low, wet land where water collects   f bridge

7 a line of water, on the surface of the ocean, that moves   g canal

1 **Look. What plants can you see?**

2 **What is the article about? Circle.**

- cacti around the world
- how nature can help technology
- ways of cooking and eating cacti

The Future Is ... *Cacti*??

Can you imagine living in a desert and not drinking for a year? **A cactus could!**

There are around 2,000 types of cacti. They come in many different shapes and sizes. Some are round and some are flat. Some are shaped like stars. Some are smaller than your finger. Giant ones are taller than three giraffes! In the Americas, you can find cacti all the way from Patagonia at the southern end of South America up to Canada in the north. There is even an "island" of cacti on a salt "lake" in Bolivia.

Cacti are amazing! They can survive in very dry habitats. When it rains, they collect water and keep it. They can live on this water for many years. Scientists found water inside a cactus eight months after it died! People have survived in the desert by drinking water from cacti.

You can eat the fruit of some cacti. You can also eat the green parts of some cacti, like prickly pears. In Mexico, you can buy cacti in the grocery store!

Hundreds of years ago, people in Mexico discovered that boiled prickly pears could clean water. Recently, scientists in Florida have done experiments to learn how. They found the parts of the cactus that could clean dirty drinking water. Now, they are trying to use cacti to clean ponds and swamps.

Cacti can teach us about conserving water, too. They can collect water from fog. Scientists in China are studying the skins of cacti to find out how cacti collect water. They are using technology to collect water from the air in the same way. This technology would be very useful during water shortages.

Cacti could be really important for our planet's future!

3 Read and put the main points in the order they appear in the article. Write 1–4.

Main Points

_____ Some types of cacti can clean dirty water.

_____ There are many different shapes and sizes of cacti.

_____ Cacti can teach us about conserving water.

_____ Cacti are amazing at surviving in very dry habitats.

4 Match the supporting evidence below to the main points above. Write 1–4.

Evidence

a Cacti can collect and store water for many years. _____

b Scientists in Florida have done experiments to find out how. _____

c Some are smaller than your finger, but the giant ones are taller than three giraffes. _____

d Scientists are building machines that collect water from the air in the same way as cacti. _____

5 Read the statements and circle *T* (true) or *F* (false).

a There are 200 different types of cacti. **T   F**

b Cacti grow in North and South America. **T   F**

c You will die if you drink water from cacti. **T   F**

d You can eat and cook some kinds of cacti. **T   F**

e People in Mexico have recently discovered that prickly pears can clean water. **T   F**

f Scientists in China are using technology to collect water from the air. **T   F**

g Cacti can only survive in wetlands. **T   F**

h Some scientists are studying how cacti collect water from fog. **T   F**

6 Read and answer.

a Have you ever eaten cactus? _____

b If so, did you like it? If not, would you like to? _____
_____

Before/after/when/as Clauses

Before **there was a bridge**, we used to take a ferry.
I played soccer after **I finished my homework.**
When **it rains**, cacti collect water and store it.
You were singing as **you were doing your homework.**

1) **Circle.**

a **Before / When** the land is dry, food can't grow.

b **Before / As** the Aztecs built Mexico City, there was a swamp there.

c **Before / After** they built the canal, it was much easier to travel from coast to coast.

d We had a fantastic time sightseeing **after / when** we went on vacation.

e They ran up the beach **after / as** the waves came in, so they didn't get wet!

2) **Complete.**

after   when   before   as   after   when

a _____ I got into bed, I brushed my teeth.

b I'll meet you _____ I finish my homework.

c _____ you swim in a river, you should be very careful.

d My dad wears glasses _____ he reads.

e Our friends arrived _____ the movie started.

f Sara was calling me _____ she was getting on the bus.

3 **Choose the correct verb tenses to complete the sentences.**

1 When you _____, we _____ go straight to the beach.

   a will arrive, will go   **b** arrive, will go   **c** will arrive, go

2 After the Egyptians _____ ditches, irrigation of the fields _____ better.

   a dug, will be   **b** dug, was   **c** dig, was

3 As I _____ down the road, I tripped and _____ into the ditch.

   a was running, fell   **b** ran, was falling   **c** was running, was falling

4 Dan _____ much better after he _____ lunch.

   a felt, was having   **b** felt, had   **c** was feeling, was having

5 We always _____ to the movies when we _____ my cousins.

   a go, visited   **b** went, visit   **c** go, visit

4 **Combine the two sentences. Use *before*, *after*, *when*, or *as*. Use each word once. Keep the information in the same order.**

a It rained. The plants started to grow.

   _____

b We arrived on the island. We had a picnic.

   _____

c They couldn't cross the river. The bridge opened.

   _____

d I was walking out of the ocean. A big wave hit me.

   _____

My Life

Complete the sentences to make them true for you.

a Before I went to bed last night, I _____.

b As I was going to school this morning, I _____.

c When I got to school today, I _____.

d After lunch, I _____.

1 Say and write the words. Underline *kn* or *wr*.

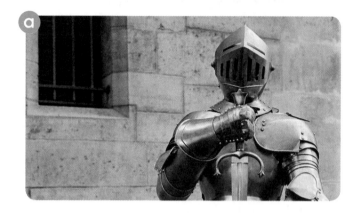

_____

_____

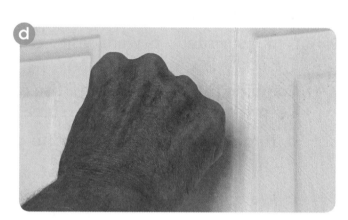

_____

_____

2 Circle the word that starts with a silent letter.

a kite   night   knight   d wrap   rap   water

b no   know   nose   e ring   wrong   wing

c rice   right   write   f knife   nice   kind

Oracy

1 Read. Circle two things that good speakers do when they are giving a presentation.

- make eye contact with the audience
- ask the audience questions
- look at the floor
- read from your paper
- don't smile
- wave their arms around a lot

Verbs with Countable and Uncountable Nouns

When you write, think about whether or not you can count the nouns.
Countable nouns can be singular or plural. When we use them, we use the appropriate singular or plural verb form:

a canal / some canals
There is a canal **in Panama.** It connects **the Atlantic and Pacific Oceans.**

a swamp / some swamps
There are some swamps **in Florida.** They have **different wetland habitats.**

Most uncountable nouns do not have a plural form. When we use them with verbs, we use the singular verb form:

some water   **There** is **water all over the world.** It is **a valuable resource.**

1) **Circle.**

a In some places, rice **grow / grows** on terraces.

b The rivers **flood / floods** every year.

c I think coffee **smell / smells** delicious!

d Water shortages **is becoming / are becoming** more common.

e The storm **was / were** very loud.

f Help! Water **is going / are going** everywhere!

2) **Look. Complete with _is_ or _are_ and _a_ or _some_.**

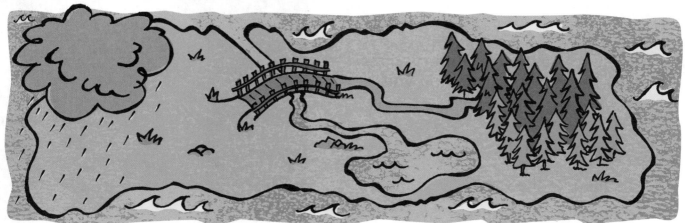

a There _____ forest.

b There _____ trees.

c There _____ bridge.

d There _____ waves.

e There _____ rain.

f There _____ salt water.

1 READ Answer the question.

Do you have to use glitter?
Which words/phrases tell you?

_____

2 PLAN Prepare to write instructions for a water picture. Complete the graphic organizer.

> **What kind of picture are you going to make?**
> _____
> _____

What equipment do you need?
_____
_____
_____
_____
_____

What do you need to do?
_____
_____
_____
_____
_____

3 WRITE Use the graphic organizer to write your instructions in your notebooks.

4 EDIT Did you ...

☐ number the steps?

☐ include imperatives?

☐ list the things you need?

☐ use countable and uncountable nouns correctly?

How to Make a Tornado in a Jar

Materials:

a jar   water
soap   food coloring
vinegar   glitter (optional)

What do you need to do?

1   Fill the jar with water so that it is ¾ full.

2   Pour some soap into the jar, and add a few drops of food coloring.

3   Add a teaspoon of vinegar to the mix. (You can also add some glitter if you want.)

4   Screw the lid back on the jar.

5   With both hands, hold the jar tight and move it around in circles as fast as you can. After a short time, you will see a tornado form!

Ready to Read: Fiction

1 Key Words 4 **Circle.**

1   The _____ wasn't working, so we didn't have any water.

    a paradise **b** pump **c** wasteland

2   Pollution made the _____ dirty.

    a monsoon **b** root **c** water supply

3   We filled ten _____ of water.

    a containers **b** deer **c** monsoons

4   Many plants—like cacti—store water in their _____.

    a dirt **b** roots **c** containers

5   After the storm, there was _____ all over the car.

    a deer **b** wasteland **c** dirt

6   After the _____, the river was very full.

    a monsoon **b** paradise **c** container

2 **Complete.**

> erode deer wasteland dirt paradise container

a   I've never been anywhere so beautiful—this place is _____!

b   Floods are causing the land to _____.

c   After the trees disappeared, the area became a _____.

d   We saw a frightened _____ hiding in the forest.

e   Can you bring a water _____, please?

f   The children had _____ on their faces after playing in the yard.

1 **Look. What kind of weather do you think the story is about?**

2 **Read. Was your answer to Activity I right?**

Reading Strategy: Sequencing

When we read, it's important to understand the order (sequence) of events in a story. Look for sequence words and time expressions that may help.

The Calm Before the Storm

Olivia drank another glass of water. The temperature was climbing. It was becoming more uncomfortable every day. She looked out the window at the yard. It was looking more and more like a desert wasteland. There were lifeless plants and dry, brown grass. It was like this every year before the monsoon season. Olivia wanted the rain to come, but she didn't want the storms to come.

As she looked at the garden, she started thinking. In school, they learned that the word *monsoon* comes from an Arabic word, *mausim,* meaning "season" or "wind change." It was certainly a season of changing winds. Last year, a very sudden strong wind knocked down a tree and blew her trampoline into her neighbor's yard. Sometimes, the winds were so strong that they destroyed houses.

The thing Olivia liked least about the monsoon was the dust. When the wet winds from the Gulf of Mexico blew over the hot desert landscape, they carried sand and dirt from the desert.

It could be difficult to see. She remembered two years ago when they were driving home from her aunt's house. There was so much dust. They had to move off the road, and they sat in the car for two hours before it was safe to drive again!

The best thing about the monsoon, though, was the feeling after it stopped. When the sun shone through the clouds and the air was cooler, it felt like paradise. There was often a beautiful smell, too. The whole town smelled like fresh flowers.

As Olivia put down the glass, she noticed that the sky was changing color.

"Mom, I think we need to close the windows … "

SB pages 149–154

3 Circle the sequencers and time expressions.

a It was becoming more uncomfortable every day.

b It was like this every year before the monsoon season.

c The best thing about the monsoon, though, was the feeling after it stopped.

d Last year, a very sudden strong wind knocked over a tree and blew her trampoline into her neighbor's yard.

e Sometimes, the winds were so strong that they destroyed houses.

f She remembered two years ago when they were driving home from her aunt's house.

g As she looked at the yard, she started thinking.

h They sat in the car for two hours before it was safe to drive again!

4 What happened when? Complete.

dust   cooler air   yard looks like wasteland   strong winds
difficult to see   fresh smell   dry, brown grass
sun shines through clouds   lifeless plants

Before the Monsoon	During the Monsoon	After the Monsoon

Had to (Obligation in the Past)

I had to **stay inside during the storm.**

She had to **fix the broken pump to get a drink.**

We had to **conserve water when there was a water shortage.**

There was so much dust that they had to **move off the road.**

He didn't have to **pay to cross the bridge—it was free.**

We didn't have to **get up early on the weekend.**

They didn't have to **fly— they took the train.**

1 Circle.

a There was no milk, so she **had to / didn't have to** buy some.

b There was plenty of time, so they **had to / didn't have to** hurry.

c The show was very popular, so we **had to / didn't have to** reserve tickets.

d After the storm stopped, we **had to / didn't have to** stay indoors.

e The museum was really close, so they **had to / didn't have to** take a taxi.

f I forgot my swimsuit, so I **had to / didn't have to** miss the swimming lesson.

2 Match.

1 That's very kind—you didn't   a to finish my homework project.

2 I couldn't go to the party because I had   b have to bring a gift.

3 It rained a lot, so we   c had to pay for the boat trip.

4 When he broke his arm, he   d didn't have to go to bed early.

5 When we visited the island, we   e didn't have to water the garden.

6 During school vacation, I   f had to go to the hospital.

3 **Complete with *had to* or *didn't have to*.**

a The garden was very dry, so we _____ water the plants.

b There was no spelling test this week, so I _____ study spelling words.

c She woke up late, so she _____ run to school!

d On vacation, I _____ to do any homework.

e When the water supply ran out, they _____ drink bottled water.

f The museum was free, so we _____ pay to go in.

4 **Write three sentences with *had to* and three with *didn't have to*.**

When Charlie was three, …

✓
go to bed earlier
hold his mom's hand in the street
take swimming lessons

✗
go to school
help with chores
look after the dog

a _____

b _____

c _____

d _____

e _____

f _____

5 **Write sentences that are true for you.**

a Write two things you had to do when you were five.

_____

_____

b Write two things you didn't have to do when you were five.

_____

_____

1 **Look and complete.**

	Does this conserve water?	Do I/ we do this?
Taking short showers		
Filling your bathtub to the top		
Fixing a broken faucet		
Filling your dishwasher instead of doing the dishes in the sink		
Doing only small loads of laundry		
Collecting the water from your shower		

2 **Who is conserving water? Look and mark ✓.**

3 **Why is conserving water important?**

_____

_____

_____

Check Your Oracy!

1 I used the phrases on the cue cards.
All of them / Some of them / None of them

2 I interacted with the audience during my talk.   **Yes / No**

3 I made eye contact during my talk.
All the time / Some of the time / Never

How can we use water better?

The Big Challenge

1 **Color the stars to give yourself a score.***

I thought of ideas for conserving water.	☆☆☆☆☆
I thought of solutions to use water efficiently.	☆☆☆☆☆
I helped to plan the presentation.	☆☆☆☆☆
I practiced presenting my group's idea(s).	☆☆☆☆☆
I presented my group's idea(s) to the class.	☆☆☆☆☆
I listened to the other groups' presentations.	☆☆☆☆☆

*(5 = Awesome! 4 = Pretty good, 3 = OK, 2 = Could be better, I = Needs more work!)

2 **Which idea did you like best? Why?**

_____

_____

The Big Question and **Me**

Because of the things I have learned in this unit,

1 I will _____ .

2 I will _____ .

SB page 157

1 **Circle.**

 a It hasn't rained for a long time—we need to **conserve / involve** water.

 b There's a **wetland / water shortage**—turn off the faucet!

 c Some animals live in **agriculture / fresh water** habitats.

 d Washing and cooking can both **involve / conserve** water.

 e **Water shortage / Agriculture** is the main industry in this area.

 f In dry areas, farmers use rivers for **wetland / irrigation**.

2 **Complete.**

> bridge   dam   swamps
> waves   canal   island

 a _____ can be very powerful.

 b You have to cross a _____ over the river to get to my house.

 c The ship went through the Panama _____ .

 d Cuba is an _____ in the Caribbean Sea.

 e The Aswan _____ helps to control the River Nile.

 f Alligators often live in _____ .

3 **Cross out the word you can't use.**

 1 There was a problem with the _____ , so we couldn't get a drink.

   a paradise   **b** pump   **c** water supply

 2 _____ can store water.

   a Containers   **b** Roots   **c** Deer

 3 The land was just _____—there were no plants.

   a dirt   **b** monsoon   **c** wasteland

 4 _____ can move water from one place to another.

   a Pumps   **b** Roots   **c** Paradise

 5 There were some _____ under the tree.

   a monsoons   **b** deer   **c** roots

4) Complete.

> before   as   after   when   before   when

a It started to rain just _____ I was walking out of the house.

b _____ the movie finished, they went out for pizza.

c _____ I washed my hands, I turned off the faucet.

d We watered the plants early in the morning _____ it got too hot.

e I always eat ice cream _____ I go to the beach.

f _____ they built the bridge, we couldn't drive to the island.

5) Complete with *had to* or *didn't have to* and the verb in parentheses.

Last year, there was a water shortage in my town. We all 1 _____
(conserve) water. For example, I 2 _____ (share) a bath with my
younger brothers and sisters! Luckily, I 3 _____ (share) a room with
them, too—I have my own room. Mom and Dad didn't take baths. They
4 _____ (take) very short showers. We saved the water from the bath to
water the plants. We 5 _____ (water) the garden early in the morning,
when it was cooler. Luckily, it was during the vacation, so we 6 _____
get up early—my dad watered the garden!

6) Complete with the singular or plural form of the present simple.

a Roman bridges _____ (be) amazing!

b Rain _____ (erode) the surface of the Earth.

c Water sometimes _____ (cause) a lot of damage.

d The canal _____ (go) from one coast to the other coast.

e Waves _____ (crash) onto the beach when it's windy.

f People _____ (need) water to survive.

g Some deer _____ (live) in the desert.

SPEAKING MISSION

1) **What did they say? Complete the conversation.**

> matter   sink   complaint   moment   room number
> faucet   available   fixed   help   plumber

Receptionist	Reception. How can I **1** _____ you?
Chloe	I have a **2** _____ to make.
Receptionist	Sure. What's the **3** _____ ?
Chloe	The **4** _____ is leaking in the **5** _____ .
Receptionist	OK ... let me see if I can find the **6** _____ . One **7** _____ , please.
Receptionist	I'm sorry. The plumber isn't **8** _____ now. I can send him up to your room this afternoon. What is your **9** _____ ?
Chloe	I'm in Room 504.
Receptionist	Thanks. We'll get it **10** _____ as soon as possible.

2) **Match.**

1	I have a		a	available now.
2	What's the		b	mind ...?
3	The faucet is		c	a problem with ...
4	I'm sorry. The plumber isn't		d	blocked.
5	The bathroom is		e	complaint to make.
6	There seems to be		f	there in ten minutes.
7	Would you		g	matter?
8	The plumber will be		h	flooded.
9	There is no		i	leaking.
10	The drain is		j	hot water.

3) **Have you ever had to make a complaint? What was the problem?**

_____

_____

What can you remember about ... Unit 7?

1 What kind of habitat is this?

_____

2 Which word is NOT a verb? Cross it out.

valuable   involve   conserve

3 Complete.

This is a type of _____ that carries water.

4 What is this? Circle.

ditch   dam   canal

5 What is this?

_____

6 Underline.

The island was beautiful—like a tropical **wasteland / container / paradise!**

7 Complete with *Before, After, When,* or *As.*

_____ they built the canal, ships couldn't cross Central America.

8 Mark ✓ the correct sentence.

a After the storm, the garden flooded. We had to water the plants! ☐

b After the storm, the garden flooded. We didn't have to water the plants! ☐

Read and circle.

9 **Irrigation** is / are **very important for agriculture.**

10 **When it rains, the ditch** fill / fills **with water.**

Check your answers in the Student's Book. How did you do?
10 ☐ Wow!   8–9 ☐ Great!   6–7 ☐ Good!   0–5 ☐ Try harder!

? 😃 **Why is water important?** Write your answer to the Big Question.

_____
_____
_____

8 How do numbers shape our lives?

1 ▶ 8.1 **Watch the video. Write the main idea. Then, complete the graphic organizer.**

> measure distances   Roman numerals   shape of pine cones
> storm clouds   combination locks   the Pirahã system

Main Idea: _____		
How We Use Numbers	Fibonacci Sequences	Ways of Counting

2 **Add one more detail to each column.**

3 Key Words 1 **Complete.**

> sequence   numerals   equals   quantity   combination   distance

a

This is a _____ lock.

b

This helps you to measure _____ .

c

She is measuring _____ .

d

This is a _____ of numbers.

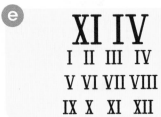
e

XI IV
I II III IV
V VI VII VIII
IX X XI XII

These are Roman _____ .

f

Two plus two _____ four.

1 Key Words 2 **Look and match.**

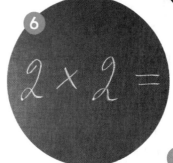

a trick

b formula

c cube

d symmetry

e multiply

f chessboard

g diagonal

2 **Circle.**

1 A _____ is a mathematical rule.

   a trick **b** formula **c** cube

2 Rubik's _____ were very popular in the 1980s.

   a cubes **b** chances **c** chessboards

3 To make ten, you can _____ two by five.

   a doubling **b** equal **c** multiply

4 In a word search, words can go across, down, or in a _____ line.

   a chessboard **b** diagonal **c** symmetry

5 You should take an umbrella—there's an 80% _____ of rain today.

   a chance **b** zero **c** formula

6 Surprise your friends with this amazing _____!

   a cube **b** symmetry **c** trick

1 **Look at the title and the pictures. What do you think the article is about?**

2 **Read. Mark the correct conclusion.**

Hearing and Seeing Math!

Math is everywhere. Have you ever thought about how math connects to other subjects? When you hear drumbeats in music, that's math! When you see shapes, patterns, sequences, and symmetry, that's math, too!

Do you enjoy dancing or clapping to music? Music usually has a pattern of beats. Different types of music around the world have different patterns. African and Indian music is very different from Western music. To follow the beat, musicians have to recognize the pattern. They also need to count!

Languages also have patterns of beats. Knowing where the "beats" are in words and sentences can help us to understand a language. It can help other people to understand us, too! Different languages are different in how they distribute "strong" and "weak" beats in words and sentences.

Have you seen Pablo Picasso's paintings? You can see cubes and other shapes in some of them. But many of his paintings look "unnatural." Picasso broke the rules of symmetry and math. He painted parts of shapes that you don't normally see together. In one painting, you can see the front and back of a violin at the same time!

Some paintings by modern artists are like chessboards of color. Others are single shapes in one color. Piet Mondrian used straight black lines and just three or four colors in his paintings. You can see some of the smaller shapes double and multiply to make bigger shapes.

a So, if you want to be good at math, you should listen to more music and look at more paintings! ☐

b So, in music, in language, and in art, math is all around us. If you look and listen, you'll see it and hear it everywhere! ☐

c So, if you want to be good at art, languages, or music, you need to be good at math! ☐

3 **Read and match the main points with the evidence that supports them.**

Main Points

1 You can hear math in music. _____

2 You can hear math in languages. _____

3 Many of Picasso's paintings look "unnatural." _____

4 You can see math in modern artists' paintings. _____

Evidence

a He broke the rules of symmetry and math.

b It usually has a pattern of beats.

c Some of the smaller shapes double and multiply to make bigger shapes.

d Knowing where the beats are in a sentence can help us to understand.

4 **Write one more piece of evidence from each paragraph.**

1 _____

2 _____

3 _____

4 _____

5 **Read and answer.**

a Which painting in the article do you like best? Why?

_____

_____

b Look at the paintings below. Which one do you think uses math? Why?
Write two sentences about it.

_____

_____

Verb + Gerund

Some verbs can be followed by a gerund. For example:
recommend, enjoy, remember, imagine, suggest, and avoid.

I remember seeing **an amazing magician.**

Can you imagine painting **like that?**

She enjoys dancing.

He avoids doing **chores.**

We recommend visiting **the Picasso museum.**

They suggest arriving **before lunch.**

1 **Circle.**

a I **recommend / avoid** watching the movie—it's awesome!

b Do you **enjoy / imagine** studying math? I do—I love it!

c Mom **remembered / suggested** going to the doctor. I think it's a good idea.

d I can't **suggest / imagine** being able to do tricks like that!

e My grandpa **remembers / recommends** going to school when he was a boy.

f They stood under a tree to **enjoy / avoid** getting wet.

g He is allergic to peanuts, so he **enjoys / avoids** eating them.

h Can you **recommend / imagine** visiting Patagonia? It would be amazing!

i I **suggest / don't like** giving bad news.

2 **Complete with the correct form of the verb.**

> be   order   practice   do   have   use   check   win   drink

a I really enjoy _____ puzzles—it's lots of fun!

b Do you remember _____ that math competition? You were awesome!

c I recommend _____ you have everything you need.

d I can imagine _____ a big 15th birthday party.

e Dad can't sleep. He should avoid _____ coffee in the evening.

f They suggest _____ a pen and paper to work out the math problem.

g My great-grandmother remembers _____ the first girl on a soccer team at her school.

h I suggest _____ the macaroni and cheese. It's delicious!

i You don't like _____ piano. You prefer playing soccer.

3 **Look and complete. Use a gerund.**

They enjoy _____ .

You must avoid _____ at the sun—it's dangerous!

I can remember _____ in the ocean on vacation.

He suggested _____ the instructions.

4 **Complete the sentences. Use a verb and a gerund from the words in parentheses.**

a Do you _____ an umbrella? (suggest / take)

b Can you _____ a new mathematical formula? (imagine / invent)

c My sister _____ chess. (enjoy / play)

d Doctors _____ healthy foods. (recommend / eat)

My Life

Complete the sentences with a gerund to make them true for you.

a I enjoy _____ on the weekend.

b I remember _____ when I was on vacation.

c I don't like _____ .

d I avoid _____ because _____ .

1 Say and write the words. Underline the silent letters *gh*, *g*, *b*, or *l*.

a

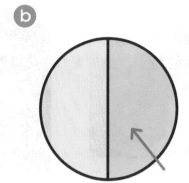
b

c
___ ___ ___ ___ *(verb)*

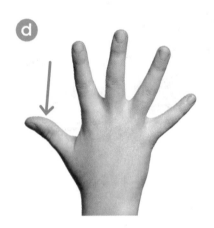
d

e
___ ___ ___ ___ *(verb)*

f

2 Circle the word that DOESN'T have a silent *gh*, *g*, *b*, or *l*.

a	comb	bulb	thumb	d	bright	bigger	frightened
b	talk	calf	only	e	wild	walk	talk
c	big	sign	design	f	lamb	climb	cabin

1 Read. Circle three things that good speakers do when they are giving a presentation.

- speak clearly
- ask "Can everyone hear me?"
- speak very quickly
- ask "Can you listen, please?"
- speak very, very slowly
- ask "Do you have any questions?"

Although

We can use *although* at the beginning or in the middle of a sentence. It contrasts two different ideas. We use a comma to separate the two ideas.

Although **the project was easy, it took a long time.**

I enjoy math, although **it's sometimes difficult.**

1) **Match.**

1 Although they were late,

2 I ate the food,

3 Although he doesn't like math,

4 People celebrate birthdays all over the world,

5 The project was interesting,

6 Although she speaks Spanish,

a although it wasn't very tasty.

b although it wasn't easy.

c they didn't miss the bus.

d she thinks Portuguese is difficult.

e he passed the exam.

f although the celebrations are different.

2) **Rewrite the sentences with *although*.**

a The computer was new, but it didn't work.

Although _____.

b He enjoyed playing with the Rubik's Cube, but he couldn't solve it.

_____, although _____.

c Math tricks are fun, but they can be difficult!

_____, although _____.

d Chess is over 1,000 years old, but it's very popular.

Although _____.

e They were tired, but they wanted to play.

Although _____.

f I was hungry, but I was too tired to eat.

_____.

g He thinks spiders are very interesting, but he's afraid of them.

_____.

Writing

1 **READ** **Answer the question.**

What can butterflies tell us about?

_____

_____

2 **PLAN** **Prepare to write a letter about something you did at school. Complete the graphic organizer.**

Who to? _____

What about? _____

What did you do?

_____

_____

_____

Why did you do it?

_____

_____

_____

3 **WRITE** **Use the graphic organizer to write your letter in your notebook.**

4 **EDIT** **Did you ...**

☐ include an address?

☐ include the date?

☐ include a greeting?

☐ end with a closing?

396 Main Street, Santander

September 16

Dear Grandma,

How are you? It's fun being home again, although I miss you a lot!

I want to tell you about a project I did this week at school with my new science teacher, Ms. Barros. It's a really cool wildlife survey. You can join in, too! You have to go to the website bugcount.com and enter your location. Then, you spend a few hours counting butterflies near where you live. Butterflies can tell us a lot about changes in the environment. Scientists use the information we collect to learn more about where different kinds of butterflies live and how the number of butterflies is changing. Although it takes a while, it's really important.

I found:

4 green caterpillars

3 small brown and orange butterflies

2 big white butterflies

1 beautiful bright blue butterfly

I took some photos, and Ms. Barros helped me identify the species on the Internet.

Let me know what you find in your garden!

Love,

Lottie

150

1 **Key Words 4** **Complete.**

Across

1 You see this on the ground when the sun is behind you.

2 You use this for digging.

3 This is a measurement—around 2.5 cm.

4 You can tell the time with this—when it's sunny!

5 You can get power from this.

6 You can _____ time, distance, and quantity.

Down

1 You can put this on your wall to decorate it.

2 Buildings are made from this hard, gray material.

3 This describes metal that has become red or brown because water has reacted with air.

4 This is a measurement— around 30 cm.

2 **Complete.**

> socket   shadow   shovel   concrete   measure   sundial

a Our patio is made of _____ .

b When Dad was digging in the garden, he dropped the _____ on his foot!

c Could you help me _____ this table, please?

d Is there a _____ in here? I need to charge my tablet.

e You can't use a _____ when it's cloudy!

f The dog was trying to play with its own _____!

1 Look. What do you think the story is about?

_____

2 Read. Circle the best alternative title for the story.

All About Ancient Egypt   An Unusual Homework Project   Clocks Through History

Reading Strategy: Paraphrasing

> Paraphrasing is putting sentences into your own words.
> Paraphrasing shows you understand what you read.

You Can Count on Me!

"Really?!" said Sophia. "A human sundial?"

"Yes," replied Maria, "I know Mr. Clarke gave us instructions for making one from a paper plate, but I'm planning do something much cooler. I'll need your help, though. Then, it could be a joint project."

Sophia looked at Maria. They were best friends because they enjoyed similar things. They both liked art, and they loved to design amazing, unusual creations. They were studying the ancient Egyptians. Their vacation homework project was to recreate an Egyptian invention.

"OK …" said Sophia. "What exactly are you thinking?"

"So, you know that the Egyptians were one of the first cultures to measure time?" continued Maria.

"Uh-huh."

"Well, before they invented small sundials, they used giant shadow clocks to tell the time. They used the position of the shadows to figure out the time."

"I know. So why don't we just use a big stick or a shovel to make a shadow?"

"Because the patio is made of concrete! We need to use something that can stand without help—like you!"

"Riiiight. So what do we have to do?"

"So at noon, we go out into the yard. You need to stand with your back to the sun. Then, I'll put a rock on the line where your shadow falls, and write '12' on it."

"And then?"

"We do the same thing at one o'clock, then every hour until the sun goes down. You have to stand in the same place every time, though. And then, when you stand in that same place tomorrow, we'll be able to tell the time."

"But how do we set the time for the morning?"

"Oh, yes, I forgot to say. We need to get up when the sun rises, and …"

"Uh-oh. You're on your own for that part!" laughed Sophie.

3 Read the paraphrased sentences below. Then, underline the corresponding sentences in the text in the correct color.

a But you will need to help me.

b They had to make a model of something the Egyptians invented.

c They figured out the time from where the shadows were.

d I need to use something that won't fall over.

4 How could you paraphrase these sentences from the story? Mark ✓ the best option.

1 "I'm planning to do something much cooler."

    a "I can't understand the instructions." ☐

    b "I have a more interesting idea." ☐

2 "So, you know that the Egyptians were one of the first cultures to measure time?"

    a The Egyptians used clocks before many other cultures. ☐

    b The Egyptians invented clocks. ☐

3 Before they invented small sundials, they used giant shadow clocks to tell the time.

    a First they used giant shadow clocks, then smaller sundials. ☐

    b First they used small sundials, then giant shadow clocks. ☐

4 "Uh-oh. You're on your own for that part!"

    a "That's too early for me!" ☐

    b "Nobody wants to help you!" ☐

5 Paraphrase the sentences from the story.

a They were best friends because they enjoyed similar things. They both liked art, and they loved to design amazing, unusual creations.

_____

_____

b "We do the same thing at one o'clock, then every hour until the sun goes down. You have to stand in the same place every time, though."

_____

_____

Verb + Infinitive

Some verbs can be followed by the infinitive of another verb and some can be followed by an infinitive or a gerund.

I'm planning **to do** something much cooler.

Oh yes, I forgot **to say**!

You need **to stand** with your back to the sun.

She wants **to create** something really unusual.

We decided **to work** together.

They agreed **to make** a human sundial.

Grandpa likes **to measure** in feet and inches. / Grandpa likes **measuring** in feet and inches.

They hate **to be** late. / They hate **being** late.

1 **Circle.**

a Tom was late because he forgot **to set / setting** his alarm.

b I avoid **to work / working** too late at night.

c You need **to multiply / multiplying** three by two to equal six.

d They decided **to get / getting** some new wallpaper.

e We recommend **to save / saving** your work.

f She doesn't enjoy **to play / playing** chess.

g Mom wants us **to take / taking** piano lessons.

h My brother forgot **bringing / to bring** the map.

2 **Match.**

1 Yesterday was horrible. I'd prefer

2 Oh, no! My bike is gone. I forgot

3 That book looks interesting. I'd love

4 The two friends agreed to

5 The car is dirty. Mom is planning

6 Can you help? I need

a meet at the movie theater.

b to read it.

c not to talk about it.

d someone to bring me a shovel.

e to lock it.

f to clean it tomorrow.

3 **Complete with the correct form of the verb in parentheses.**

a We agreed _____ my cousins in town for pizza. (meet)

b Dad decided _____ pancakes for breakfast yesterday. (cook)

c I made a sundial, but I forgot _____ it to school this morning. (take)

d Tina is planning _____ math at university. (study)

e You need _____ careful not to delete your work! (be)

f Sam and Rosie wanted _____ the formula before the test. (learn)

4 **Mark ✓ the three sentences where both the gerund and infinitive can be used.**

a My sister loves _____ (play) with her Rubik's Cube. ☐

b Do you enjoy _____ (find) patterns in sequences of numbers? ☐

c We decided _____ (buy) a new car next year,
   when we can afford it. ☐

d I don't like _____ (watch) magic tricks. ☐

e She hates _____ (do) chores. ☐

f The project is optional—they don't need _____ (do) it if they don't
   want to. ☐

5 **Write the correct form of the other sentences from Activity 4.**

_____

_____

_____

6 **Write sentences that are true for you.**

a Next summer, I really want _____.

b On the weekend, I'm planning _____.

c Last week, I forgot _____.

d I decided _____.

e I love _____.

f I prefer _____.

1 **Look and complete.**

	Do you think this is a good idea?	
	Yes ✓	No ✗
Giving children under 12 years old allowance		
Buying the first thing you see		
Spending your allowance every week		
Counting your allowance so you know how much you have		
Buying something because your friend has the same thing		
Spending less on some things so you can spend more on other things		

2 **Who is managing their allowance well? Look and mark ✓.**

a — If I want to buy something, I look in two or three different stores to compare prices. ☐

b — I don't know how much money I have. ☐

c — If I want to buy something expensive, I don't buy anything else for a few weeks. ☐

d — I know what I can buy with one dollar. ☐

e — I can never buy anything expensive because I spend my allowance as soon as I get it. ☐

g — Sometimes you have to wait before you can buy something you really want. ☐

3 **Why is managing your allowance and budgeting important?**

_____

_____

Check Your Oracy!

1 I spoke clearly and at a good pace.   **Yes / No**

2 I made eye contact with my audience when speaking.
All of the time / Some of the time / Never

3 I used the phrases on the cue cards when appropriate.
All of them / Some of them / None of them

How can we use numbers to make something?

The Big Challenge

1 **Color the stars to give yourself a score.***

I thought of ideas and invented a code with my partner.	☆☆☆☆☆
I worked with my partner to write a message in our code.	☆☆☆☆☆
I broke another pair's code and read their message.	☆☆☆☆☆
I worked with my partner to write a coded reply.	☆☆☆☆☆
I presented our messages to the class with my partner.	☆☆☆☆☆
I listened to the other pairs' presentations.	☆☆☆☆☆

*(5 = Awesome! 4 = Pretty good, 3 = OK, 2 = Could be better, 1 = Needs more work!)

2 **Which code did you think was the most difficult to break? Why?**

_____

_____

The Big Question and **Me**

Because of the things I have learned in this unit,

1 I will _____.

2 I will _____.

1 Circle.

a You can see lots of examples of the Fibonacci **distance / sequence** in nature.

b I'm saving my money so I can **afford / equal** to buy a smartwatch.

c We're trying to find out the **quantity / distance** from home to school.

d You have to add the two **preceding / combination** numbers to get the next number in the Fibonacci Sequence.

e Ten plus nothing **equals / affords** ten.

f They bought a very large **numeral / quantity** of ice cream!

2 Complete.

> doubling   chessboard   zero   delete   symmetry   formula

a A _____ has 64 squares—32 black and 32 white.

b The number below one is called _____.

c You can make ten by _____ five.

d Do you know the _____ for changing feet to meters?

e Don't press that button—it might _____ all your work!

f There are some beautiful examples of _____ in nature.

3 Circle.

1 The ancient Egyptians used _____ to tell the time.

   a shovels   b sockets   c sundials

2 Before we used meters, we used feet and _____.

   a shadows   b inches   c concrete

3 You can charge your phone in that _____.

   a socket   b sundial   c foot

4 I decorated my room with really cool _____.

   a shadows   b shovels   c wallpaper

5 Oh, no—I left my bike out in the rain! It might get _____.

   a rusty   b preceding   c diagonal

8

4 **Look. What do you think the woman's job was?**

5 **Read and complete. Sometimes there is more than one correct answer. Were you right?**

Can you imagine 1 _____ (celebrate) your 100th birthday? In August 2018, Katherine Johnson celebrated hers. Katherine Johnson is a famous mathematician. When she was young, she really enjoyed 2 _____ (count). She loved 3 _____ (learn) and decided 4 _____ (study) math in college. She planned 5 _____ (work) as a mathematician.

She got a job as a "computer" at NASA, solving math problems. But she wanted 6 _____ (find out) more about NASA's work. She suggested to her managers that she go to meetings that only men went to. She needed 7 _____ (be) very determined. She remembers 8 _____ (ask) lots of questions! Her managers agreed 9 _____ (let) her move to NASA's flight research team.

Katherine's math helped to send astronauts into space and eventually to the moon!

6 **Rewrite the sentences with _although_.**

a I'm not very good at chess, but I enjoy playing it.
Although _____.

b We need a new car, but we can't really afford it.
_____, although _____.

c They broke the code, but it wasn't easy!
_____, although _____.

d The sundial is very old, but it still works.
Although _____.

SPEAKING MISSION

1 **What did they say? Complete the conversation.**

> coordinates   map   minus   obstacles   treasure   turn   x-axis   y-axis

Boy   Let's play captain and explorer.

Girl   I'll be the explorer!

Boy   I'll be the captain!

Girl   Who has the 1 _____?

Boy   I do, and it's your 2 _____ to find the treasure!

Girl   OK ... so I am starting on zero on the 3 _____ and zero on the 4 _____ . Can I move to X minus I, Y zero?

Boy   Yes, you can move there. There are no 5 _____ .

Girl   Great. Now, I want to move to X minus I, Y minus I.

Boy   Oh, no, you can't move there. There's a big volcano!

Girl   A volcano? Oh, no! OK. How about X 6 _____ 2, Y zero?

Boy   Yes, there's nothing there.

Girl   Great. I hope I'm close to the 7 _____ ... What are the 8 _____ for the treasure?

Boy   I can't tell you! You have to guess!

Girl   Can you give me a clue?

Boy   No! (laughs): I think we might be playing all night ...

2 **Match.**

1 It's your	a	x (one), y (one)?
2 Can I	b	an obstacle there. There's a/an ...
3 No, there's	c	move (four) on the x-axis and (three) on the y-axis?
4 What about	d	clue?
5 Can I move	e	turn ...
6 Can you give me a	f	to x (minus 3), y (minus 2)?

3 **Where and when might you need to read a map?**

_____

_____

What can you remember about ... Unit 8?

① Complete.

This is an example of the Fibonacci _____ in nature.

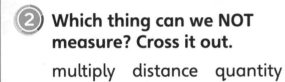

② Which thing can we NOT measure? Cross it out.

multiply   distance   quantity

③ What is this an example of? Circle.

formula   doubling   symmetry

④ What is this?

A Rubik's _____

Complete.

⑤ This is a _____.

⑥ You can tell the time by looking at the _____.

Complete with a gerund or an infinitive.

⑦ Oh, no! He forgot _____ his calculator. (bring)

⑧ I avoid _____ too much the night before a test. (study)

Write *although* in the correct place in the sentence.

⑨ I was really tired, I stayed up late to watch the movie.

⑩ They agreed to work together, they didn't know each other.

0 2 4 8 16 32 ?

Check your answers in the Student's Book. How did you do?
10 ☐ Wow!   8–9 ☐ Great!   6–7 ☐ Good!   0–5 ☐ Try harder!

? 😀 **How important is electricity?** Write your answer to the Big Question.

_____
_____
_____

9 What makes the natural world so amazing?

1 ▶ 9.1 **Complete the graphic organizer.**

> Mt. Everest   large smelly flower   Death Valley   cheetah
> mountains in Patagonia   rocks in Antelope Canyon   Antarctica
> giant redwood trees   Challenger Deep   tiny glowing creatures

Harsh Places

**The amazing
natural world**

Animals

Beautiful Places

Unusual Places

Plants

2 **Add one more example for each category.**

3 Key Words 1 **Find the words!**

> harsh   beautiful
> unusual   breathtaking
> intriguing   incredible
> impressive   exceptional

B	P	A	G	P	C	Z	K	L	I	E	E
K	R	E	N	H	P	L	U	N	H	V	X
S	V	E	R	I	A	F	T	U	S	I	C
N	H	T	A	R	I	R	R	H	P	S	E
O	Y	U	F	T	I	O	S	L	Z	S	P
B	G	C	U	G	H	G	X	H	Z	E	T
G	W	A	U	A	W	T	I	X	L	R	I
N	E	I	V	E	O	P	A	L	V	P	O
B	N	Z	D	Q	A	N	L	K	E	M	N
G	U	N	U	S	U	A	L	O	I	I	A
E	L	B	I	D	E	R	C	N	I	N	L
R	X	G	H	B	M	O	H	H	D	W	G

1 [Key Words 2] **Match.**

1 the structure of bones supporting an animal's body

2 someone who studies rocks and the history of the Earth

3 to study or research something very carefully

4 strong covering to protect the outside of someone or something

5 crocodiles, alligators, and lizards are examples of this type of animal

6 a group of rocks of the same type

7 related to the ocean

a armor

b reptile

c marine

d formation

e skeleton

f investigate

g geologist

2 **Complete.**

> formation   geologists   skeleton   reptile   marine

Mary Anning used to explore the beach and cliffs around Lyme Regis.

The cliffs are part of a limestone 1 _____ that contains a lot of fossils. Mary's family used to sell the fossils to 2 _____.

One day, Mary found some bones. They were part of the 3 _____ of a 4 _____ 5 _____ called an ichthyosaur.

1 **Look. Do you know the names of any of the places? Where do you think they are?**

Reading Strategy: Monitoring and Clarifying

Sometimes when we read a text, there are words that we don't understand. When we can't figure out what the words mean from the rest of the text, we can look them up in a dictionary.

2 **Read and circle any words you don't know.**

CHOCOLATE ROCKS!

Have you ever seen rocks that look like chocolate? Or pancakes? Or lakes of salt? There are examples of unusual rock formations all over the world. Let's take a look …

When you look at these hills, what do you see? There are over 1,000 of these small limestone hills on the island of Bohol, in the Philippines. The biggest ones are 120 m high. Only grass grows on them. In the dry season, the grass turns brown—and that's what gives them their name: the Chocolate Hills! This intriguing rock formation confuses geologists— they can't agree on exactly how the hills formed.

If the Chocolate Hills are making you feel hungry, how about visiting the Pancake Rocks? They're in Punakaiki, on the South Island of New Zealand. They look like stacks of giant pancakes—yum! Like the Chocolate Hills, they are made from limestone. They started forming around 30 million years ago, when the skeletons of dead marine animals fell to the seabed. Over time, a lot of mud and clay fell on top of them and squashed them. Eventually, earthquakes lifted the seabed out of the ocean. This formed the cliffs and coast that are there today.

Would you prefer something less sweet and more salty? You could take a trip to the Salar de Uyuni in Bolivia, high in the Andes mountains. It's the Earth's largest salt flat, covering more than 10,000 km^2. This breathtaking formation looks a bit like a giant mirror. You might feel like you're walking in the air! It formed when some ancient lakes joined together and then dried up. Although it's a harsh, desert environment, a few exceptional plants and animals survive here. They include pink flamingos, rare hummingbirds, and ancient cacti.

3 Look at the words you circled. Which ones can you figure out from the context? Write them in the chart below. Then, write the words you need to look up in the dictionary.

Words I Can Figure Out from Context	Words I Have to Look Up in the Dictionary

4 Underline these words in the text. Then, match them with their definitions.

1 confuse
2 stack
3 seabed
4 squash
5 flamingo

a the bottom of the sea
b a type of bird
c to make something flat, using weight
d to make someone feel uncertain
e some things one on top of another

5 Read the statements and circle *T* (true) or *F* (false).

a The three rock formations are all in the same country.   T   F
b Geologists are not certain about how the Chocolate Hills formed.   T   F
c The Chocolate Hills and the Pancake Rocks are made of limestone.   T   F
d The Pancacke Rocks were the result of a volcano.   T   F
e The Salar de Uyuni salt flats are not at the same level as the sea.   T   F
f Nothing lives in the Salar de Uyuni.   T   F

6 Read and answer.

a What is the most impressive natural thing you have seen?

_____

b What was amazing about it?

_____
_____

Quantifiers

A few **exceptional plants and animals survive here.**

There is little **life in such a harsh environment.**

There aren't many **plants in the desert.**

There isn't much **water in the lake.**

There are a lot of **limestone hills.**

A lot of **mud fell on top on them.**

Are there any **fossils on the beach?**

There hasn't been any **rain there for years!**

1 **Put the quantifiers in the correct column.**

> any   a few   little   much   many   a lot of

With Countable Nouns	With Uncountable Nouns	With Countable and Uncountable Nouns

2 **Circle.**

a There were **much / many** small dinosaurs, as well as big ones.

b There isn't **much / many** rain in the desert.

c Paleontologists have found **a lot of / much** fossils in Chile and Argentina.

d There has been very **few / little** snow there in the last ten years.

e Do you have **any / many** idea why this animal has armor?

f There are **few / little** places in the world as impressive as the Salar de Uyuni.

SB page 188

3 **Complete with the correct quantifier.**

> any   a few   little   much   many   a lot of

a How _____ money have you saved?

b There is very _____ need for an umbrella in the desert!

c Some reptiles are endangered—there aren't _____ of them left.

d Beaches can be great places to study geology—you can find _____ interesting rocks there.

e Hurry up! The bus leaves in _____ minutes!

f Do you have _____ pets?

4 **Look and complete with *any*, *little*, *much*, *many*, or *a lot of*. Use each quantifier once.**

a Are there _____ fossils on the beach?

b Yes, there are _____ fossils.

c Are there very _____ geologists?

d Yes, there are _____ geologists investigating the fossils.

e Is there very _____ sun?

f No, there's very _____ sun.

My Life

Complete the sentences to make them true for you.

a I did a lot of _____ on vacation.

b I have a few _____.

c There aren't many _____ at my school.

d I don't eat much _____.

e I don't have any _____.

1 Color all the words that sound the same in the same color.

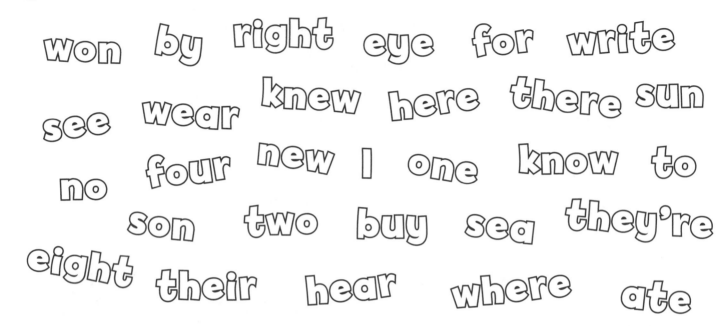

won   by   right   eye   for   write
see   wear   knew   here   there   sun
no   four   new   I   one   know   to
son   two   buy   sea   they're
eight   their   hear   where   ate

2 Circle.

a   You'll need to **wear / where** a hat **wear / where** you're going!

b   We bought ice cream **for / four for / four** people.

c   Did she tell her **son / sun** to stay out of the **son / sun**?

d   Freddie doesn't feel well. He **ate / eight ate / eight** cookies!

e   Oh, no! **I / Eye** think I got something in my **I / eye**.

f   Could you ask them to put **their / there** things over **their / there**?

Oracy

1 Read. Underline the three main reasons for visiting Ngorongoro.

One of the greatest natural wonders in the world is Ngorongoro Conservation Area in Tanzania, in Africa. You should visit Ngorongoro for many reasons! First of all, you can see the world's largest volcanic crater. It's huge, and it's over 2 million years old! Also, there is a museum that has ancient human fossils. You can see footprints of ancient humans that are millions of years old! Finally, you can see all kinds of wild animals: rhinos, hippos, lions, cheetahs, zebras, and even pink flamingos. The animals run completely free. It's an amazing place! I recommend that you visit it soon.

Stative Verbs

Stative verbs describe a state that lasts for a while instead of an action. Stative verbs are not usually used in progressive forms. We can use them to talk about permanent situations.

She has **an older brother.** (stative verb)

The fossils are **from Chile.** (stative verb)

We are investigating **this formation.** (action verb)

We can also use them to talk about some temporary situations—often to describe thoughts, opinions, and feelings.

I think **deserts are beautiful.** (stative verb)

He doesn't like **caves.** (stative verb)

Do **you** agree **with me?** (stative verb)

1 **Circle.**

a My grandparents **are / are being** from Argentina.

b **Do you have / Are you having** any brothers or sisters?

c The geologist **looks / is looking** very closely at the reptile's skeleton.

d **I love / am loving** swimming in the waves.

e Look! They **swim / are swimming** close to the cliffs!

f I **don't remember / am not remembering** dates very well.

2 **Complete with the verbs in parentheses. Put stative verbs in the present simple and action verbs in the present progressive.**

a I _____ (want) to climb a mountain one day.

b He _____ (climb) very quickly at the moment.

c We _____ (like) playing chess.

d My brother and sister _____ (disagree) about what to watch on TV all the time!

e _____ you still _____ (watch) that show? It's very long!

f My cousin _____ (be) very brave.

g They _____ (not have) a lot of time to do their homework.

1 READ **Answer the question.**

What does this animal eat? _____

> This animal is a mammal, but it doesn't have fur. Some kinds live in the ocean, and others live in rivers. Occasionally, they swim next to ships and boats and jump high into the air. They find the fish they eat by using echoes underwater. They make high-pitched clicking sounds. Then, the sounds bounce back from the fish. When the sounds bounce back, these animals hear them in their throats! The most common types are gray, but all types are very intelligent.

2 PLAN **Prepare to write a descriptive paragraph about another animal. Complete the graphic organizer.**

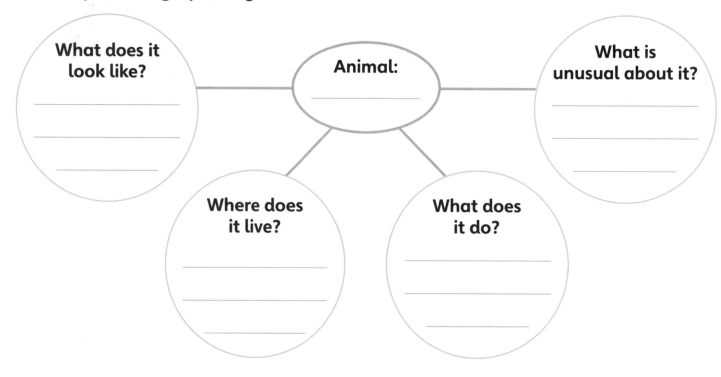

3 WRITE **Use the graphic organizer to write your descriptive paragraph in your notebook.**

4 EDIT **Did you ...**

- ☐ include information about the animal's appearance?
- ☐ include information about the animal's actions?
- ☐ describe what is unusual about the animal?
- ☐ use stative verbs correctly?

1 Key Words 4 **What are they? Write.**

> beard   warrior   giant   fist   thumb   fierce

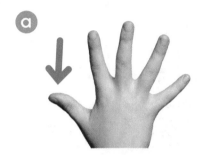
a

_____

b

_____

c

_____

d

_____

e

_____

f

_____

2 **Circle.**

1 There are many different Native American _____ .

   a fists **b** tribes **c** beards

2 The two groups were _____—they used to compete a lot.

   a giants **b** thumbs **c** rivals

3 They didn't see the lion—it was _____ in the long grass.

   a lurking **b** doubling **c** investigating

4 The _____ was very big and tall—taller than a house!

   a beard **b** giant **c** thumb

5 Tom is really _____—he kept running after he broke his foot!

   a tough **b** fierce **c** harsh

6 Dad is growing a _____ for the winter.

   a thumb **b** fist **c** beard

1 **Look. What do you think the giant is doing?**

2 **Read. Was your answer to Activity I correct?**

Reading Strategy: Understanding Characters

> As you read a story, ask yourself questions about the characters. Ask: What words can I use to describe the characters? What does this person do and why?

The Story of Atlas

The Ancient Greeks believed that the sky was round, like the Earth. That's why, in pictures, it often looks like Atlas is holding up the Earth.

In Ancient Greece, many, many years ago, lived a tribe of giants called the Titans. They were the children of the Earth and the sky.

Atlas led the Titans in a war with their rivals—the Olympians. Although Atlas was strong and brave, the Titans lost. Zeus, who was the leader of the Olympians, punished Atlas by making him stand at the edge of the Earth and hold up the sky. Despite his strength, he sweated and strained under the sky. Though he was learning a lot about the stars and the planets that he could see, he was getting bored.

One day, Heracles visited Atlas. Heracles was another Greek hero. He was having trouble finding some golden apples, so he needed some help. "Hi, Atlas. How are you? You must be very tired," he said. "Yes," Atlas replied, "I am." "I can hold up the sky for a while, if you'd like." Heracles said. "Really? I'd love to stretch my legs and take a break," said Atlas hopefully. "Sure, no problem. But do you mind doing me a small favor?

Please find some golden apples," said Heracles. So Heracles held up the sky while Atlas went to find the apples. Atlas enjoyed being free from the weight of his punishment. So, when he returned, he didn't want to hold up the sky again. Heracles promised he would continue the job. But, he said, "Just let me get a cushion to make myself more comfortable." "Okay, sure," said Atlas and took back his place under the sky. Heracles, laughing, took the golden apples and never returned.

Another hero, Perseus, came by. He had recently killed a monster. "Hi, Atlas. Nice day! I wonder if I could get a bed for the night and perhaps a little food, too." With that, Atlas growled, "I am not a hotel. Can't you see how hard I'm working?" When Atlas refused to help, Perseus became furious. He pulled out Medusa's head and showed it to Atlas.

With one glance at the monster's face, Atlas turned to stone. And that is how he became a range of mountains—the Atlas Mountains in North Africa.

3 Write the words in first column. Then, write your guesses in the second column.

	Example from the Text	What We Can Guess About the Character
Atlas's Thoughts/ Feelings/Words		
Atlas's Actions		

4 How are Heracles and Perseus similar and different? Complete the graphic organizer.

Heracles	Heracles and Perseus	Perseus

5 Choose either Heracles or Perseus. Write a sentence to describe his character.

6 Think and write.

Can you think of ...

a an ocean that is named after Atlas?

b a reason a book of maps is called an atlas?

Relative Pronouns

Zeus, who was the leader of the Olympians, punished Atlas.
Those are the mountains where Atlas turned to stone.
He was learning a lot about the stars and planets that he could see.

(1) **Match.**

1 Would you like one of the cookies   a   where we buy our food.

2 That's the supermarket   b   that he took of the rocks.

3 A geologist is someone   c   who I know from gymnastics.

4 He showed us some photos   d   where they found the fossils.

5 I just saw my friend   e   that I baked?

6 We're going to the beach   f   who studies the structure of the Earth.

(2) **Complete with *who*, *where*, or *that*.**

a My birthday was a day _____ I will never forget!

b Dad bought some milk for the woman _____ lives next door.

c That's the place _____ I was born.

d Like birds, reptiles are animals _____ lay eggs.

e That's the geologist _____ the dinosaur is named after.

f We live on a block _____ people are very friendly.

3) Order the words to make sentences.

a   a giant / was / turned to stone / who

Atlas _____ .

b   where / lives / the house / my cousin

That's _____ .

c   mammals / fur / are / don't have / that

Dolphins _____ .

d   a hero / Atlas / was / who / visited

Perseus _____ .

e   were / found / millions of years old / bones / that

Diego _____ .

4) Join the two sentences by using *who*, *where*, or *that*.

a   Finn MacCool was a warrior. He lived in Northern Ireland.

_____

b   Birds are animals. They have feathers.

_____

c   We're going to a beach. You can swim with dolphins.

_____

d   The giant had a beard. It was longer than a man.

_____

e   We went to a museum. They have a lot of fossils.

_____

5) Write sentences that are true for you. Use *that*, *who*, and *where*.

a   My school is a place _____

_____ .

b   My best friend is someone _____

_____ .

c   _____ is something

_____ I really enjoy.

1 **Look and complete.**

	Is this good for the natural world? Yes ✓ / No ✗	Do I/my family do this? Yes ✓ / No ✗
Eating food that has traveled a long way		
Using renewable energy		
Taking short showers		
Cooking more food than you need		
Refilling a water bottle instead of buying a bottle of water		
Walking or cycling instead of driving		

2 **Who is taking care of the natural world? Look and mark ✓.**

3 **Why is taking care of the natural world important?**

_____

_____

_____

Check Your Oracy!

1 I structured my talk around a main idea with sequence words.   **Yes / No**

2 I spoke clearly at a good pace.   **All of the time / Most of the time / Sometimes**

3 I convinced my classmates to visit the natural wonder I talked about.   **Yes / No**

What makes the natural world so amazing?

The Big Challenge

1 **Color the stars to give yourself a score.***

I thought of natural wonders with my partner.	☆☆☆☆☆
I discussed and agreed on a natural wonder to present with my partner.	☆☆☆☆☆
I researched information to include in our plan.	☆☆☆☆☆
I worked with my partner to make a plan.	☆☆☆☆☆
I worked with my partner to write/design our plan.	☆☆☆☆☆
I presented our plan to the class, with my partner.	☆☆☆☆☆
I looked at/listened to the other pairs' presentations.	☆☆☆☆☆

*(5 = Awesome! 4 = Pretty good, 3 = OK, 2 = Could be better, I = Needs more work!)

2 **What did your classmates think were the best ideas in your plan?**

_____

_____

The Big Question and **Me**

Because of the things I have learned in this unit,

1 I will _____.

2 I will _____.

177

SB page 201

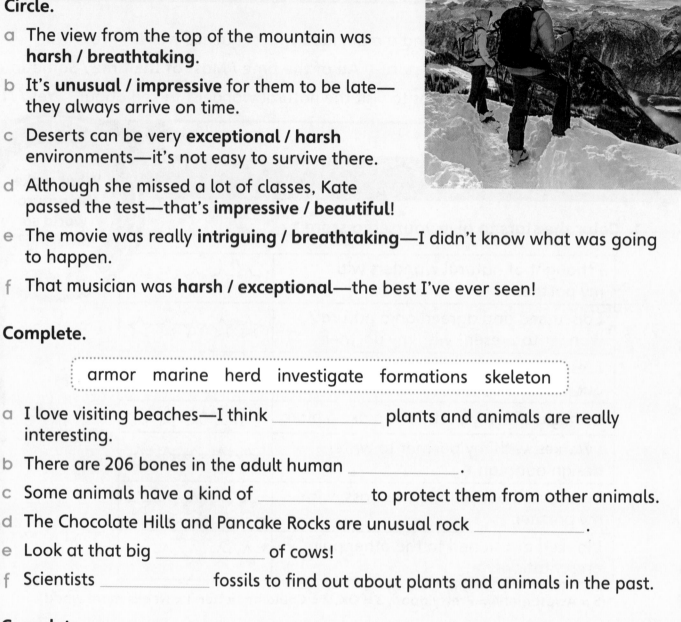

1 **Circle.**

a The view from the top of the mountain was **harsh / breathtaking**.

b It's **unusual / impressive** for them to be late—they always arrive on time.

c Deserts can be very **exceptional / harsh** environments—it's not easy to survive there.

d Although she missed a lot of classes, Kate passed the test—that's **impressive / beautiful**!

e The movie was really **intriguing / breathtaking**—I didn't know what was going to happen.

f That musician was **harsh / exceptional**—the best I've ever seen!

2 **Complete.**

> armor   marine   herd   investigate   formations   skeleton

a I love visiting beaches—I think _____ plants and animals are really interesting.

b There are 206 bones in the adult human _____.

c Some animals have a kind of _____ to protect them from other animals.

d The Chocolate Hills and Pancake Rocks are unusual rock _____.

e Look at that big _____ of cows!

f Scientists _____ fossils to find out about plants and animals in the past.

3 **Complete.**

> beards   warriors   thumb   giants   fierce   rivals

There are many stories about 1 _____. They are always big and strong, but they have very different personalities. Some are kind and gentle, like Paul Bunyan. Others are 2 _____, scary 3 _____, like Finn MacCool. Some have lots of hair and long, hairy 4 _____, like Benandonner. Finn and Benandonner were 5 _____—they both thought they were the strongest! Finn tricked Benandonner by sucking his 6 _____ and pretending to be a baby!

9

4 Circle.

Could you be a geologist?

Do you know **1 any / little** geologists?
Geologists study the surface of the Earth.
They have to spend **2 a lot of / many** time
outdoors.

Geologists also study natural processes like
earthquakes and floods. To do this, they
need to study **3 a few / much** other sciences
like physics, chemistry, biology, and math.

Geologists study the history of the Earth, too. Sometimes, there is **4 many / little**
information available. They investigate fossils of ancient plants and animals. There
aren't **5 much / many** other jobs where you get to dig in so **6 much / many** dirt!

5 Complete with *that*, *who*, or *where*.

a The biggest bone came from a dinosaur _____ was 40 meters long.

b Diego was with his parents, _____ were both geologists.

c The desert is a harsh environment _____ few animals can survive.

d The dinosaur had armor _____ protected it from other dinosaurs.

e Ngorongoro is a place _____ you can see the world's largest volcanic
crater.

f Benandonner ate some stone cake he got from Oonagh, _____ was
Finn's wife.

6 Complete with the verbs in parentheses. Put stative verbs in the present simple and action verbs in the present progressive.

a I _____ (think) caves are really intriguing.

b They _____ (look) at the rocks on the beach now.

c She _____ (not remember) where she left her bag.

d Look! He _____ (throw) stones into the ocean.

e _____ you _____ (understand) the homework?
I don't!

f Don't disturb us—we _____ (work) on our project.

1 **Read and answer.**

a Who were the main characters in your story?

_____

b Where did you set your story?

_____

c What happened ...

at the beginning of your story? _____

_____

in the middle of your story? _____

_____

at the end of your story? _____

_____

2 **When would you use the phrases? Write *a*, *b*, or *c*.**

> a interacting with the audience
> b interacting with the presenter
> c organizing a talk

1 Can you repeat that? ____

2 Can everyone hear me? ____

3 First of all, ____

4 Can you speak more slowly? ____

5 Finally, ____

6 Do you have any questions? ____

3 **What did you say? Write an example.**

1 organizing the information in your story

_____

2 interacting with the audience when giving your presentation

_____

3 interacting with the presenter while watching a presentation

_____

Wrap-up

What can you remember about ... Unit 9?

① **Unscramble the letters to make two words that mean the same as *amazing*.**

b c d e e i l i n r   i_____ e

p s s e e v i i m r   i_____ e

② **What is this?**

an unusual rock

_____

③ **Which one does NOT protect an animal? Cross it out.**

spike   armor   reptile

④ **Circle.**

Ichthyosaurs were **marine / combined / breathtaking** reptiles. They lived in the ocean.

Complete.

Finn MacCool was a
5_____. He was
the leader of the Fianna
   6_____.

Circle.

⑦ There are **much / any / a lot of** incredible places in the world.

⑧ **Complete with a relative pronoun.**

Mary Anning was a girl

_____
found a fossil skeleton.

Complete with the stative in the present simple or an action in the present progressive form of the verb in parentheses.

⑨ The glowworms _____

(be) breathtaking.

⑩ Here, they
_____
(dangle) silk threads to catch insects.

Check your answers in the Student's Book. How did you do?

10 ☐ Wow!   8–9 ☐ Great!   6–7 ☐ Good!   0–5 ☐ Try harder!

? 😃 **What makes the natural world so amazing?** Write your answer to the Big Question.

_____

_____

_____

181

All About Oracy!

Unit I: Ground Rules

Oracy rules help make our presentations and discussions more effective.

1 How about ...?

2 That's important.

3 That's not important.

Unit 2: Recognizing and Respecting the Feelings and Views of Others

We listen to and respect our classmates' opinions, even when we don't agree.

4 That's a good point!

5 Yes, but ...

6 Do you agree?

Unit 3: Asking Questions to Get Further Information and Clarity

We can ask questions to find out more information or to check our understanding.

I have a new pet.

Can you repeat that?

7 What does X mean?

8 Why? Because ...

9 Can you repeat that?

Unit 4: Expressing Opinions

It's important to participate in a discussion by saying your opinion and agreeing and disagreeing with others.

10 I think ...

11 I agree because ...

12 I disagree because ...

Unit 5: Participating in a Discussion and Eliciting Contributions from Others

When we have a good discussion, we ask others for their opinions and invite them to talk, too.

6 Do you agree?

13 What do you think?

Unit 6: Giving Evidence to Support an Argument

I think we should bring burgers and fries. What do you think, Jack?

Well, I disagree because …

To make a strong argument, it's important to give information supporting your opinion.

11 **I agree because …**

12 **I disagree because …**

14 **For example, …**

15 **I think X is important because …**

Unit 7: Speaking in Front of an Audience

When you speak in front of an audience, it's important to make eye contact. Good speakers often ask their audience questions during a presentation and thank them, too.

16 **Is everyone ready?**

17 **Do you have any questions?**

18 **Can everyone hear me?**

Unit 8: Speed and Clarity of Delivery

When you give a presentation, it's important to think about how fast and how clearly you speak. Try to speak clearly and not too fast so that people can understand you more easily.

18 **Can everyone hear me?**

19 **Can you speak more slowly?**

20 **Can you speak up?**

Unit 9: Organizing and Structuring a Talk

To make it easy to understand a talk or presentation, organize your ideas and use sequencers.

21 **First of all,**

22 **Also,**

23 **Finally,**

Acknowledgments

The authors and publishers acknowledge the following sources of copyright material and are grateful for the permissions granted. While every effort has been made, it has not always been possible to identify the sources of all the material used or to trace all copyright holders. If any omissions are brought to our notice, we will be happy to include the appropriate acknowledgments on reprinting and in the next update to the digital edition, as applicable.

Key: U = Unit.

Photography

All the images are sourced from Getty Images.

U1: Belen Majdalani/PhotoAlto Agency RF Collections; JamieGrill; JillLehmannPhotography/Moment; kali9/E+; Westend61/Germany; HillStreetStudios/DigitalVision; Anna Erastova/iStock/Getty Images Plus; ANTONYDICKSON/Staff/AFP; DinodiaPhotos/HultonArchive; ucielang/iStock/Getty Images Plus; juststock/iStock/Getty Images Plus; wmaster890/iStock/Getty Images Plus; TimHawley/Photolibrary; Creativ Studio Heinemann; xxmmxx/iStock/Getty Images Plus; Westend61; oxygen/Moment; SamBassett/TheImageBank; 10'000 Hours/DigitalVision; LaneOatey/BlueJeanImages; STEFANOLUNARDI/iStock/Getty Images Plus; 3DSculptor/iStock/Getty Images Plus; U2: PandaWild/iStock/Getty Images Plus; Historical/CorbisHistorical; Bettmann; PhotoQuest/ArchivePhotos; ValeryBrozhinsky/iStock/Getty Images Plus; julos/iStock/Getty Images Plus; 10'000 Hours/DigitalVision; SimonMcGill/Moment; AlexandraGrablewski/TheImageBank; AndrewPini/StockFoodCreative; BiwaStudio/Stone; DorlingKindersley; JustinSullivan/Staff/GettyImagesNews; DaveAlan/E+; SciencePhotoLibrary-NASAEARTHOBSERVATORY/BrandXPictures; Apic/RETIRED/HultonArchive; elenabs/iStock/Getty Images Plus; Lev Savitskiy/Moment; Arctic-Images/DigitalVision; JohnPhillips/Stringer/GettyImagesEntertainment; PaulMarotta/GettyImagesEntertainment; StocktrekImages; Stockbyte; NASA/Handout/ArchivePhotos; AntonioM.Rosario/TheImageBank; CLAUSLUNAU/SciencePhotoLibrary; Prasit photo; U3: zokara/E+; Bettmann; CR Shelare/Moment; AlexanderNewcomer/EyeEm; HeroImages; imagenavi; DorlingKindersley; AntonPetrus/Moment; BarbaraBergmann/EyeEm; Daisy-Daisy/iStock/Getty Images Plus; Nick David/DigitalVision; PeterCade/TheImageBank; PhonlamaiPhoto/iStock/Getty Images Plus; monkeybusinessimages/iStock/Getty Images Plus; MikeKemp; AdieBush/Cultura; Joe Fox/Photographer's Choice/Getty Images Plus; blackdovfx/iStock/Getty Images Plus; Noctiluxx/E+; Keystone-France/Gamma-Keystone; MirageC/Moment; AlexanderSpatari/Moment; RichardNewstead/Moment; Donald Iain Smith; triocean/istock/Getty Images Plus; U4: Hero Images; Saran_Poroong/iStock/Getty Images Plus; DougalWaters/DigitalVision; 5second/iStock/Getty Images Plus; Axel Bueckert/EyeEm; Fuse/Corbis; PHILIPPEDESMAZES/AFP; NickBallon/TheImageBank; MassanPH/Moment; AnatolyM/iStock/Getty Images Plus; TierUndNaturfotografieJundCSohns/Photographer'sChoice; undefinedundefined/iStock/Getty Images Plus; DorlingKindersley; Elizabethsalleebauer/RooM; Jose Luis Pelaez Inc/DigitalVision; Stanislav Krasilnikov/TASS; undefined/iStock/Getty Images Plus; Sidekick/E+; KarunyapasKrueklad/EyeEm; PunsayapornThaveekul/EyeEm; JeffreyCoolidge/DigitalVision; SuparatMalipoom/EyeEm; SrdicPhoto/E+; Westend61; ClausChristensen/DigitalVision; HillStreetStudios/DigitalVision; BRULOVE/iStock/Getty Images Plus; JennyDettrick/Moment; suedhang/ImageSource; Hero Images/DigitalVision; U5: LittleHandImages/Moment; stocktributor/iStock/Getty Images Plus; Daniel Bosworth/British Tourist Authority; CreatiVegan.net/Moment; belchonock/iStock/Getty Images Plus; Westend61; PatrickWalsh/EyeEm; SofieDelauw/Cultura; iaravenanzi/DigitalVision; rhkamen/Moment; DEA/J.E.BULLOZ/DeAgostini; SteveAllen/Photolibrary; AndreyGorulko/iStock/Getty Images Plus; Batke/iStock/Getty Images Plus; JonKopaloff/Stringer/FilmMagic; SergioDionisio/Stringer/GettyImagesNews; Paket/iStock/Getty Images Plus; SongsakWilairit/EyeEm; DianaMiller/Cultura; FeifeiCui-Paoluzzo/Moment; MarkLStanley/DigitalVision; shomos uddin/Moment; Richard T. Nowitz/Corbis NX/Getty Images Plus; MintImages-TimRobbins/MintImagesRF; AnthonyBoccaccio/TheImageBank; peepo/E+; Lauz83/iStock/Getty Images Plus; UniversalImagesGroup; ChakarinWattanamongkol/Moment; PaulBradbury/OJOImages; Kryssia Campos/Moment; Alexander Spatari/Moment; SusannaWyatt/AWLImages; TinaFields/E+; AugustineChang/iStock/Getty Images Plus; neyro2008/iStock/Getty Images Plus; ac_bnphotos/E+; hanohiki/iStock/Getty Images Plus; fitopardo.com/Moment; japatino/Moment; U6: JoseFusteRaga/CorbisDocumentary; ChristopherStevenson/TheImageBank; Westend61; SolStock/iStock/Getty Images Plus; Steven Puetzer/Photographer's Choice/Getty Images Plus; DigiPub/Moment; Timmary/iStock/Getty Images Plus; icefront/iStock/Getty Images Plus; esemelwe/E+; kicsiicsi/iStock/Getty Images Plus; Morsa Images/DigitalVision; SummerK Photography/Moment; Andyworks/iStock/Getty Images Plus; MangoStar_Studio/iStock/Getty Images Plus; Suradech14/iStock/Getty Images Plus; Watcharinpanyawutso/iStock/Getty Images Plus; TARIKKIZILKAYA/iStock/Getty Images Plus; EkaterinaSmirnova/Moment; ma-k/iStock/Getty Images Plus; Jean-philippe WALLET/iStock/Getty Images Plus; kadmy/iStock/Getty Images Plus; HeroImages; marilyna/iStock/Getty Images Plus; ArielSkelley/DigitalVision; heinteh/iStock/Getty Images Plus; Ekely/iStock/Getty Images Plus; AndreaLong/EyeEm; yelet/iStock/Getty Images Plus; ThongchaiSaisanguanwong/iStock/Getty Images Plus; HotHibiscus/iStock/Getty Images Plus; WalterB.McKenzie/Stockbyte; subjug/iStock/Getty Images Plus; BetsieVanderMeer/Stone; U7: Matthew Davidson/EyeEm; Didier Marti/Moment; Andrew Williams/EyeEm; pawel.gaul/E+; mattpaul/RooM; RuudMorijn/iStock/Getty Images Plus; Hein von Horsten/Gallo Images; Karen Fox/Image Source; Sittipong Yongthaisong/EyeEm; Westend61; aja84/iStock/Getty Images Plus; miu_miu/iStock/Getty Images Plus; Feargus CooneyLonely Planet Images/Getty Images Plus; Monkey Business Images/Stockbyte; Elke Hesser/Corbis; wlablack/iStock/Getty Images Plus; Sebastien Lemyre/EyeEm; duckycards/E+; robeo/iStock/Getty Images Plus; Bernard Castelein/Nature Picture Library/; Shaun Egan/Photographer's Choice/Getty Images Plus; J. Parsons/Moment Open; HRAUN/E+; ideabug/E+; seanscott/RooM; John Seaton Callahan/Moment; andresr/E+; ultraforma_/E+; Bertll23/iStock/Getty Images Plus; Ekaterina Nosenko/Moment; Tim Graham/Getty Images News; abalcazar/E+; Farm Images/Universal Images Group; U8: Fernando Trabanco Fotografía/Moment; Anfisa Kameneva/EyeEm; PeopleImages/iStock/Getty Images Plus; Jeffrey Coolidge/The Image Bank; ChubarovY/iStock/Getty Images Plus; Stockbyte; VikramRaghuvanshi/E+; serts/iStock Unreleased; Jrg Lcking/EyeEm; sanyal/iStock/Getty Images Plus; Wavebreakmedia/iStock/Getty Images Plus; Alex Walker/Moment; Vladimir Godnik; Peter Dazeley/Photographer's Choice; biriberg/E+; Brian Spranklen/Taxi; Photo 12/Universal Images Group; borojoint/iStock/Getty Images Plus; De Agostini/M. Carrieri/Getty Images Plus; Ales-A/iStock/Getty Images Plus; ridvan_celik/E+; Wavebreakmedia/iStock/Getty Images Plus; Nophamon Yanyapong/EyeEm; monkeybusinessimages/iStock/Getty Images Plus; Chillim/iStock/Getty Images Plus; Hero Images; YaroslavKryuchka/iStock/Getty Images Plus; Plattform; Feifei Cui-Paoluzzo/Moment; SvetaP/iStock/Getty Images Plus; Adrian Peacock/Stockbyte; bowdenimages/iStock/Getty Images Plus; Jose Luis Pelaez Inc/DigitalVision; Craig Tuttle/Corbis Documentary/Getty Images Plus; Kris Connor/WireImage; Donaldson Collection/Michael Ochs Archives; photovideostock/E+; www.lmvphoto.com/Moment; serts/iStock Unreleased; Science Photo Library; Slow Images/Photographer's Choice/Getty Images Plus; U9: MRI805/iStock/Getty Images Plus; Alan Copson/AWL Images; Dorling Kindersley; Afriandi/Moment; Kim Andelkovic/500Px Plus; Pakawat Thongcharoen/Moment; holgs/E+; Sierralara/RooM; dasar/Moment; jonnysek/iStock/Getty Images Plus; YaroslavKryuchka/iStock/Getty Images Plus; ballyscanlon/DigitalVision; Hero Images; Tetra Images - Wim van den Heever/Brand X Pictures; Yuji Karaki/DigitalVision; alessandroguerriero/iStock/Getty Images Plus; Detroit Free Press/Tribune News Service; kasto80/iStock/Getty Images Plus; jankovoy/Getty Images Plus; Ridofranz/iStock/Getty Images Plus; Inti St Clair/Tetra images; Richard Newstead/Moment; Stockbyte; Fuse/Corbis; Emma Gibbs/Moment Open; Cavan Images/Cavan; 117 Imagery/Moment; DieterMeyrl/E+; Daniel Sambraus/EyeEm; Andersen Ross Photography Inc/DigitalVision; Zen Rial/Moment; Dean_Fikar/iStock/Getty Images Plus; Corey Ford/Stocktrek Images; MarcelStrelow/iStock/Getty Images Plus.

Illustrations

Andrew Painter; Carlos Velez; Dan Widdowson; Diego Funck; Emmanuel Urueta; Graham Ross; Ria Maria Lee.

Cover illustrations by Alessia Trunfio (Astound).